Y0-CCU-405

105725

JAMES B. DUKE MEMORIAL LIBRARY
JOHNSON C. SMITH UNIVERSITY
CHARLOTTE, N. C. 28216

RESUMES
for EXECUTIVES
and PROFESSIONALS

RESUMES
for EXECUTIVES
and PROFESSIONALS

Maury Shykind

ARCO PUBLISHING, INC.
NEW YORK

Portions of this book were previously published under the titles *Resumes for Job Hunters* and *Self-Marketing Manual for Executives*.

Third Edition, First Printing, 1984

Published by Arco Publishing, Inc.
215 Park Avenue South, New York, N.Y. 10003

Copyright © 1984, 1976, 1971 by Maury M. Shykind

All rights reserved. No part of this book may
be reproduced, by any means, without permission
in writing from the publisher, except by a
reviewer who wishes to quote brief excerpts in
connection with a review in a magazine or
newspaper.

Library of Congress Cataloging in Publication Data
Shykind, Maury.
   Resumes for executives and professionals.
   Rev. ed. of: Self-marketing manual for executives.
1971.
   1. Résumés (Employment) I. Title.
HF5383.S54   1984   650.1′4   83-3753
ISBN 0-668-06102-2   (Reference Text)
ISBN 0-668-05779-3   (Paper Edition)

Printed in the United States of America

Contents

RESUMES
for EXECUTIVES
and PROFESSIONALS

Introduction

Obviously, you purchased this book because you are either presently unemployed or desirous of making a change of position. Circumstances beyond your control may be the reason for not being employed. Forced lay-offs due to reduced sales volume or mergers wherein your services were no longer required, are the chief causes for high unemployment in business and industry.

Since there are many persons seeking employment in your field, job competition becomes very considerable. However, the individual who has the better knowledge to compete against other applicants, will have the advantage in obtaining a position. By acquiring the experience and know-how in exposing himself in the job marketplace, he will be one of the fortunate few who is effective in his search.

This fact also applies to the individual who, for one reason or another, is unhappy, frustrated, blocked-in or "plateaued" in his present position and, therefore, is seeking a change. (*Note*: The wise individual will remain in his present position, no matter how distasteful it may be, until his search is concluded.)

(Note: this book is directed to both sexes. The male designation will be applied for easier reading, thereby avoiding the continuous "his/her" usage.)

The self-marketing methods explained and recommended herein, have proven highly successful in a great many instances. The book will illustrate, advise and counsel in the development, organization and implementation of a personal marketing campaign through step-by-step procedures. The pitfalls and barriers to be avoided will be reviewed throughout. Interview and negotiation techniques as well as evaluation of offers will be discussed.

Once a position has been obtained, chapters on how to procure job longevity and induce a reduction of stress on the job are also included.

The style of communication is informal and conversational, as though the reader were sitting across the desk from a career consultant in a face-to-face session. It is hoped that the personal touch will make the subject matter so easily understood that practically all questions a reader may have will be answered as the program progresses through its various stages. Follow-through and execution of the advice and counsel offered will become simple and easy, resulting in a successful solution to the job problem, as well as a realization of individual career objectives.

Maury Shykind

Preface

The unemployed or employed individual who enters the job marketplace immediately becomes a "product," but usually fails to realize this fact. He goes about seeking a position on a hit-or-miss basis without a specific marketing program to reach every "sales" outlet available for the "product"—himself.

He lacks the know-how to expose himself and his abilities to the best advantage. This is no reflection on his capabilities. He has had few jobs to date and certainly never made a profession of seeking a position 8 hours a day, 5 days a week. He is, undoubtedly, very knowledgeable in his own line of work, but is really a novice when it comes to searching for a job.

As a result, he doesn't have a clear understanding of the many accesses available to obtain an interview and is unfamiliar with successful interview techniques. Where the company will ask every conceivable question about the prospective employee, he, in turn, rarely interviews the prospective employer in any great depth. Not knowing how to negotiate, the starting compensation, in many instances, is usually less than what he could have received.

Selling yourself is no different from selling any other product! First, *you need to know the product* (yourself) as expertly as your own line of work. If you were selling ashtrays, you would be able to answer any question about them without stopping to think. You would look the buyer straight in the eye when you spoke to him. You must do likewise when selling yourself, without any hesitancy in your voice or actions.

Second, *you should know your sales outlets* available for your product. Referring again to the ashtray salesperson, his marketing channels would be wholesalers, jobbers, distributors, dealers and any other large quantity buyers. Actually, there are 12 sales outlets where you can expose your product—yourself—to the greatest number of prospective employers. (See page 27.)

Third, knowing the product and where it can be "sold", *you need to know how to sell it.* You should know how to glamorize, dramatize or romanticize it in a manner which will create a desire for the product without lying about it. And above all, you must show the company that they can make a good profit from it. No matter what your salary range may be, the prospective employer takes many factors into consideration such as office or work space, a secretary, miscellaneous expenses, etc. He must realize a profit from your services, whether in a "staff" (office) or "line" (operational) job, else he doesn't need or cannot afford you.

The book, therefore, is divided into three major parts:

1. Determination of realistic job goals, both immediate and long-range.
2. Development of a marketing program to fit your needs.
3. Implementation of a marketing campaign to obtain a position.

There are added chapters on:

1. Longevity and Advancement
2. Job-Related Stress

In essence, you will find out:

Who you are; what you should be doing; for whom you should be doing it; where you would do it best and enjoy it the most.

Individuals who will utilize the ideas, suggestions and recommendations incorporated in this book should encounter little difficulty in obtaining a most meaningful, rewarding and satisfying position.

Your spouse is a very important part of your job search. Make him/her, or a friend, an accessory to the program by involving them as a "sounding board." Let them read the section on "Implementation of Marketing Campaign." You will find that they will contribute substantially, not only in evaluations, but also by participating in role-playing sessions as the program progresses.

Determination of Career Goals

SELF-ASSESSMENT

The first step in any marketing program is to know what the product is, and what it consists of in terms of both technical specifications and benefit features. A personal assessment or appraisal is therefore required. You must know who you are before you can sell yourself.

The following questionnaires should be answered factually and realistically in order to gain an insight into your own personality needs and aspirations. Your immediate or short-term career image and marketplace will become apparent in the process.

Forms to be Filled Out

1. Education
2. Work History
3. Personal
4. Evaluation of Experience
5. Career Speculation and Goals

(1)
Education

Years . . . Elementary School . . . . High School . . . . College . . . .

Colleges attended . . . .

Degrees and dates received . . . .

Other schooling, courses, or job training . . . .

. . . .

. . . .

Memberships and offices held in school organizations . . . .

. . . .

. . . .

Goals during school years . . . .

. . . .

Describe reasons for changes in goals, if any . . . .

. . . .

. . . .

(2)

CHRONOLOGICAL WORK HISTORY
(List present or most recent position first, and then work backwards)

	Name and address of company	Dates employed from - to	Earnings start - finish	Job titles start - finish	Supervisory responsibility	Reasons for leaving
(1)						
(2)						
(3)						
(4)						
(5)						
(6)						

What did you like best in:

Job No. 1 _____

Job No. 2 _____

Job No. 3 _____

What did you like least in:

Job No. 1 _____

Job No. 2 _____

Job No. 3 _____

(3)
Personal

MILITARY SERVICE—Branch. . . . . Rank or Rating. . . . . . .

What do you admire most in superiors? . . . .

In subordinates? . . . .

In associates? . . . .

What is your strongest trait as an executive? . . . .

Why do you feel you are ready for a more responsible position? . . . .

. . . .

What are you doing to improve yourself? . . . .

. . . .

Affiliations, memberships in civic or professional organizations . . . .

. . . .

Leisure activities . . . .

What starting earnings would be satisfactory? . . . .

Next year? . . . . 5 years? . . . . 10 years? . . . .

Are you willing to relocate? . . . .

What are your geographic relocation preferences? . . . .

Why? . . . .

How much time per month are you willing to travel? . . . .

Additional comments . . . .

. . . .

. . . .

(4)
Evaluation of Experience

(a) What are your reasons for desiring a change of position?

(b) With what products and product lines are you familiar?

(c) What types of management functions have you been involved in?

(d) With what processes, techniques, equipment and methods are you most familiar in your line of work?

(e) In what other areas such as hobbies, etc. have you acquired experience and skills?

(f) From which aspects of your work experience have you derived the most satisfaction?

(g) Which kinds of problems or conditions have created the most difficulties or troubles?

(h) In which areas of your work do you feel that you perform best?

(i) In which areas do you tend to be neglectful or ineffective?

(j) Of all your bosses which one did you like the most? Why?

(k) How do you think those who work or have worked for you feel about you as a superior?

(5)
Career Speculations and Goals

(a) How would you like to see your career offer greater personal satisfaction?

(b) List all the positions that based on your ability and experience you feel you are qualified to handle.

(c) In what ways would you be outstanding in each of these positions?

(d) If you were hiring yourself for employment, what abilities do you have that would make you valuable to the company?

(e) Assuming you were qualified, what are some of the jobs you would enjoy the most?

(f) Which kinds of work would you like to do if you had to change your present field or line of work?

(g) Have you ever considered going into business for yourself? If so, what type?

(h) What brought you into your particular field?

(i) What are your ultimate career goals and objectives?

(j) What do you believe are the most important factors of your background or assets to help you attain these goals?

(k) What factors might limit or block your achievement?

(l) What do you feel you will have to do to accomplish your goals?

Review your answers. If you were factual and realistic in your statements, you can evaluate your potential, abilities and motivation, as well as your weaknesses. Are you down to earth in your answers to the questions on "Present and Future Earnings?" This could be a key to whether or not you have been realistic on other questions. Observance of factual rather than fanciful answers will help you to determine a meaningful career image and objective.

The self-assessment is a logical method to learn who you are, what you should be doing, and for whom and where. For example, you could now be working for a major structured organization and getting nowhere. You may discover that you are not a politically-oriented type of individual. You feel that your work should speak for itself, rather than having to boast about it. You, therefore, belong in a small or medium-size company where your recognition and rewards are greater and come sooner because management is closer to you, and is more knowledgeable of your worth to them.

Or, you are not a small-company man where your challenges and progress may be limited, but your competitive spirit requires a large organization in order to compete against many other people for advancement.

Many other personality traits and characteristics will become evident. On the chart on page 18, jot down your strengths and weaknesses. Once you know what they are, the usage of the assets and the overcoming of the deficiencies will be valuable not only at interviews, but in your everyday work as well.

Under normal circumstances you cannot be a "generalist" in your field. You must have a "Career Image" which is actually a title to the position you are seeking. Check the help wanted ads in the *Wall Street Journal* or other papers. You will find that the greatest majority of firms list positions with titles such as "Controller," "Chief Engineer," "Public Relations Manager," "Chemist," "Administrator," etc. (*Note*: A dictionary of occupational titles, published by the Government Printing Office, is available at your library. Also, the American Management Association publishes a "Middle Management Report" which lists management titles and functions.)

On page 21, one column is headed "Desirability" and the other "Availability." Review your answers on "Evaluation of Experience" and "Career Speculations." Enter all the titles of work which you have knowledge of, under the "Desirability" heading. Then list these same positions in the order of their job prospects under the "Availability" column. (See example on page 20.)

Your Personality Traits & Characteristics

Strengths	Weaknesses
(Assets)	(Deficiencies)

Examples

Good communicator— oral and written	Feel insecure
Highly motivated	Self-critical
Leadership ability	Evasive
Politically oriented	Non-aggressive
Positive & self-confident attitude	Rigid and inflexible
Adjust readily to new situations	Introvert

Note: Each trait under "strengths" could be an antonym for "weaknesses" and vice-versa.

For instance, you may show "President of the U.S." at the top of your "Desirability" listing, but obviously you would place it at the bottom of the "Availability" column. This is an oversimplification to illustrate the necessity for a realistic order of your listings in each column.

These listings will enable you to connect the position desirability with the position availability somewhere in the middle. The compatibility of the two will suggest a first choice for the type of position best suited for your immediate or short-term career objective.

The matching of the other listings will also offer alternative positions which may influence your thinking as to additional job opportunities. Your first choice may be good for an immediate goal, whereas some of the other alternatives may be better in terms of long-range opportunities.

Check your skills again from the Self-Assessment answers. You may have capabilities which are transferrable to related or supporting industries or fields. Sometimes the background or experience of a hobby or avocational activity could reflect itself into a career goal. It is wise to examine all your knowledge and abilities in all fields by recording them under the "Desirability" and "Availability" columns.

A major revelation from this appraisal may be your discovery that you possess a uniqueness that others do not share in your field. You may speak several languages; or you have a private or commercial pilot's license; or have patents granted you; or articles published etc. This could be a very helpful plus in your marketing exposures and at interviews.

Example of Career Image

Desirability	Availability
1. President of U. S.	1. Tool Designer
2. V. P. of Engineering	2. Project Manager
3. Manager of R & D	3. Chief Engineer
4. Plant Manager	4. Plant Manager
5. Chief Engineer	5. Manager of R & D
6. Project Manager	6. V. P. of Engineering
7. Tool Designer	7. Manager of Marina
8. Manager of Marina	8. President of U. S.

Uniqueness

Patent granted

(or) Speak 3 foreign languages

(or) Articles published

(or) Very familiar with pleasure boats, etc.

Note that "Plant Manager" appears as number 4 under both "Desirability" and "Availability" and could be the Career Image. However, "Chief Engineer" and "Manager of R & D" are also very closely centered and should be considered on the basis of the individual's self-analysis.

Your Career Image

Desirability	Availability
1.	1.
2.	2.
3.	3.
4.	4.
5.	5.
6.	6.
7.	7.
8.	8.
9.	9.
10.	10.

Uniqueness

THE MARKETPLACE

Now that you have determined your Career Image (Job Title), you need to locate the marketplace for it. Before you read any further, review Summary pages 23 and 24 for examples of determining this. It will assist you in understanding how to summarize your particular marketplace.

First, check the type of industry or field in which you belong. It could be Manufacturing, Engineering, Transportation, Government, Retail, Mining, Construction, Agriculture, Services, etc.

Second, determine the type of market within the industry selected. It may be Steel, Electronics, Chemicals, Textiles, etc.

Third, a further breakdown is necessary in terms of specifics within the industry, such as Plastics, Rubber, Paper, Machine Tools, Automotive Parts, Building Products, Photographic Equipment, etc.

Fourth, based on the self-appraisal of your personality needs and requirements, should the company within the industry be a small, medium or large volume concern? What should the structure and dynamics be in terms of growth opportunities for you?

Fifth, sometimes important for job satisfaction are the geographic limitations imposed either by yourself or your family. Naturally, the larger the "universe" to which you are exposed, the greater the opportunity for obtaining the most fruitful career goal. The smaller "universe" you may decide on will offer lesser possibilities. If you desire only the environments of a metropolis (your own greater city area), then you further narrow the field until it becomes merely a "job" which you are seeking, rather than a career.

Are you a small-town, grass roots type of individual, or do you prefer the more sophisticated atmosphere of a large city? Consider also that many companies or divisions of companies are located in cities, but with suburbia nearby. Conversely, many companies are situated in rural areas, with a big city and its advantages less than 50 miles distant. Nowadays, 50 miles is a short auto ride.

Any geographic limitation you set will reduce your chances for obtaining the best offer. Incidently, the larger "universe" could conceivably produce your career offer within the very geographic area you desire. However, you can not know this unless you obtain the broadest possible exposure.

Sixth, evaluate your Long Range Objectives as outlined below.

LONG RANGE OBJECTIVES

It may inflate your ego to set a high long-range goal, but are you realistic? Are you fooling or kidding yourself? Do you honestly believe you have the qualifications for an eventual top-management role? Fine, if you do! However, your potential may be only middle-management.

Obviously, you may become a Vice-President in a small or medium size company, whereas middle-management may be your top in a large company. Do you have the inner drive, motivation and abilities to be a top-level executive?

Job satisfaction is greatly dependent on your long-range goals, but must be assessed in self-acknowledged realistic terms.

Summary

You have now determined the results of your assessment for job objectives. You have an insight as to who you are as a person, and in terms of a career. You know what you should be doing, for whom and where.

Recapitulate these factors in order to determine your marketing strategy. Here are a few illustrations:

Example 1

(Career Image) . . . . Chief Engineer
(Type of Industry). Manufacturing
(Type of Market) . . . . Chemical
(Industry Specific) . . . . Plastics
(Size of Company) . . . . Medium
(Geographic Location) . . . . Midwest
(Long Range Goal) . . . . Vice-President Engineering
                                              (Top Management)

Example 2

(Career Image) . . . . Sales Manager (Could be Asst. Sales Manager)
(Type of Industry). . . . . Manufacturing
(Type of Market) . . . . Heavy Equipment
(Industry Specific) . . . . Steam Engines, Turbines, etc.
(Size of Company). . . . . Large
(Geographic Location) . . . . Entire U. S.
(Long Range Goal) . . . . Vice President Sales
                                              (Top Management)

Example 3

(Career Image) . . . . Controller
(Type of Industry) . . . . Retail Chain
(Type of Market) . . . . Hard Lines—Soft Lines
(Industry Specific) . . . . Automotive Supplies—Appliances
—Ready to Wear
(Size of Company) . . . . Small to Medium
(Geographic Location) . . . . East Coast
(Long Range Goal) . . . . Treasurer

There may be more than one Career Image because of the alternatives. When there is more than one Career Image, then chart each one the same way. You may thus expose yourself to more than one type of industry utilizing different Career Images.

You are now ready for the Marketing Campaign.

Your Personal Factors for Marketing Strategy

(Career Image) . . . .

(Type of Industry) . . . .

(Type of Market) . . . .

(Industry Specific) . . . .

(Size of Company) . . . .

(Geographic Location) . . . .

(Long Range Goal) . . . .

- -

(Career Image) . . . .

(Type of Industry) . . . .

(Type of Market) . . . .

(Industry Specific) . . . .

(Size of Company) . . . .

(Geographic Location) . . . .

(Long Range Goal) . . . .

Your Personal Factors for Marketing Strategy

(Career Image) . . . .

(Type of Industry) . . . .

(Type of Market) . . . .

(Industry Specific) . . . .

(Size of Company) . . . .

(Geographic Location) . . . .

(Long Range Goal) . . . .

- -

(Career Image) . . . .

(Type of Industry) . . . .

(Type of Market) . . . .

(Industry Specific) . . . .

(Size of Company) . . . .

(Geographic Location) . . . .

(Long Range Goal) . . . .

Development of Marketing Program

THE STRATEGY

The immediate or short-term goal to obtain a position has now been established. "Marketing Strategy" to sell the "product" is the next step. The prime purpose of the campaign is to obtain interviews. No one will hire you by phone or through correspondence. To evaluate offers for the most meaningful position, you need to obtain many interviews. Therefore, just as any product has certain defined sales outlets to locate prospects, so do you. The marketing strategy in your case consists of the following 12 sales channels:

The Mailing

Answering Ads

Chain Referrals

Business News Items

Executive Recruiters

Employment Agencies

Advice Calls

References

Personal Contacts

Alumni Placement Organizations

Professional Societies

Situation Wanted Ads

No one can predict from which of these 12 outlets the best offer will turn up. Therefore all of them should be explored to the fullest extent.

THE MAILING

The most fruitful results will come from your mailing to a *minimum* of 100 companies addressed to a specific executive. You may contact less than 100, but the more firms you reach the greater number of responses you will receive for interviews. A minimum of 100 is considered a good sampling for this purpose. (*Note*: On occasion it may be necessary to make a second mailing of 100, if interviews resulting from the first mailing prove unproductive.)

Where and how to obtain the list of companies and names of executives is explained on page 161.

This letter for the mailing, which we will call the "Motivation Letter," is designed to create interest and a desire on the part of the recipient to meet with you. Therefore, the letter should dramatize you but must be honest in every respect. You will fall flat on your face in an interview if you have lied or misrepresented yourself.

The motivation letter should contain illustrations of your accomplishments and your potentials. In other words, prove to the company that they can make a "profit" from your efforts.

Note: How to write a motivation letter and a resume will be described later.

A resume is *not* enclosed with the motivation letter under normal circumstances. You will understand why as the strategy progresses.

Replies to the mailing usually produce a flood of responses soon after the mailing date. The quantities will then taper off gradually, and you may even receive a few replies several months later. However, we are most concerned with the immediate responses. Those responses which indicate an interest in you, we will call "positives." The others which merely acknowledge receipt of your letter can be termed "negatives." Sort all replies into the "positive" and "negative" categories.

Since we are primarily interested in the "positive," re-sort them into geographic areas. Thus you can arrange itineraries for your interviews by zones where you may meet with several companies in a few days rather than hopping around the country wasting time in extensive travel.

The "positives" will ask for more information or suggest that you phone for an interview. An executive may even phone you to arrange an interview. *A word of caution: Under no circumstance permit yourself to be interviewed on the phone.* It is too easy for the caller to cancel a possible meeting. It is also impractical to prove how you can be of service to the company while on the phone. This can only be done in a face-to-face interview.

Therefore, if too many questions are asked, say words to this effect: "Mr. Jones, I appreciate your interest in asking me these questions. However, in a personal meeting I can prove qualities and capabilities which are difficult to illustrate on the phone. Can we get together to discuss what I can contribute? Would Thursday of this week or Monday of next week be convenient?"

(*Note:* Always suggest a choice of two different days for arranging the time for an interview. This is a good "closer" to obtain agreement for the get-together. Offering a choice is a positive approach which most often generates a positive answer. Remember, your first need is to obtain interviews.)

Most of the replies will be signed by the person to whom you addressed your letter. On occasion he may turn it over to the Personnel Manager. Assuming these were "positive" letter responses requesting more information, handle them in one of three ways:

1. If the letter request is from the executive, *phone him* and suggest that in a personal interview you can furnish all the information he wants. Try to obtain the interview and use the two separate days approach as previously explained. However, if he says that he would still like more information before an interview is arranged, do not push it further but tell him you will be happy to forward your resume. Then with a short cover letter or note, mail your resume to him.
2. A letter response requesting that you phone the company definitely indicates a desire for an interview. Again, do not permit yourself to be interviewed when you place the phone call or you might change the writer's original intention for a meeting. Get the interview!
3. Should the letter response come from the personnel department, it is useless as a rule to phone the sender. With a cover letter, send two or three resumes, which can be passed around to potentially interested executives.

(*Note:* The personnel department may include an application form. *Fill it out completely.* Although the chances are slight that an opening exists, why pass up a possibility? On all application forms, the question of "Salary Requirement" should be answered "Negotiable.")

The "negatives" you receive may not all be negative in the true sense of the word. Some could be converted into "positives" if you will read between the lines. Others may claim nothing is open at present, but you may be asked to drop in when you happen to be in their vicinity. List these companies by towns or areas. Should you have an interview nearby, phone these individuals and take advantage of the chat time they mentioned. Investigate every possibility since you never know what may develop.

Companies are always planning ahead. They may have been considering the establishment of a new department, expansion of an existing operation, etc. Your letter could very well arrive at a time which would tend to jell their thinking. They may have problems, and your letter coming at the right moment could create an immediate interest in you.

ACCOMPLISHMENT STORIES

Before you can compose the resume or the motivation letter, you need to know what successes you were responsible for in your business life. The average person feels that he has had no great outstanding business accomplishments since he was "paid to do the job." This is incorrect thinking. All of us, at some time, have been commended for, and were proud of, the results of our efforts.

There are several ways to cite your "Accomplishments" in the resume. Refer to the examples of resumes starting on page 37. Read the accomplishment stories, and then, based on your experience, write the style best suited for you. However, the following method should be adopted first.

Write at least six accomplishment stories. If possible, they should be related to your "career image." Write them as you would tell them. Each story could be several pages long to be certain that no important detail is omitted. *They must contain the technical terminology normally used in your type of industry.*

Each accomplishment story should be written in three parts:

(1) What the situation or problem was at the time of your assignment. State what your title was when this occurred.
(2) What YOU did to correct or improve the existing condition. Indicate your own actual involvement and/or direct supervision.
(3) What the results were in terms of dollars and/or percentage increase; savings effected; cost of personnel reduction; etc. Use specific terms by which the accomplishment can be measured.

Take the meat of each story and condense it into *three* pithy paragraphs based on the above three parts. Write a lead title or heading for each story.

Following are six examples of actual accomplishment stories:

    I. General Management
   II. Manager of Industrial Engineering
  III. Credit Manager
  IV. Treasurer
   V. Sales Manager
  VI. Manager of Manufacturing

Example I

General Management

Turns Annual Operating Loss Into Net Profit of $110,000

Assuming charge as Vice President and General Manager of a major Fire Brick Company, I found the company in very bad financial straits. There was a $619,000 mortgage to a factoring institution with the attendant high finance costs. There was no diversification of products, and morale both in the operating and sales divisions was at an extremely low point.

I rebuilt the organization taking out the dead timber. Hiring an outstanding ceramic engineer, new products were developed. A revitalized sales organization was introduced to positive sales approaches. Market researches produced additional outlets. Employe unrest was eliminated.

As a result of these remedial actions, the indebtedness was reduced to $190,000 which was then placed in lower interest bank loans. Sales increased 40 percent, and the operating loss was soon turned into a net profit of $110,000.

Example II

Manager of Industrial Engineering

Improved Methods Reduce Lead Time 28 Percent and Labor Requirements 20 Percent

A large metal fabricating concern was encountering fierce price and delivery competition. Production was behind schedule and a major customer threatened to cancel all future business unless deliveries were accelerated. My assignment was to find a way to significantly reduce time in order to be competitive.

A study was made in detail of the que, flow and operation time from the starting activity to the shipping date of the accepted product. Another study involved the overall plant layout, scheduling process, material and work flow, equipment utilization and identification of key suppliers. My recommendations were accepted for both the improvements in methods and the required educational process involved at the group level.

Over a six-month period, lead time was reduced 28 percent and labor requirements 20 percent. The resultant accelerated deliveries remedied the major customer complaint. As a by-product, a larger percentage of the industry volume was obtained because of the greater cost-effective capacity realized.

(*Note:* This story was originally three pages long and condensed to three paragraphs.)

Example III

Credit Manager

Revitalizes Department and Reduces High Delinquency
and Bad Debts to Below Industry Average

When I became Credit Manager, the company's sales were very good, but the financial strain of heavy collection losses would put the company in great jeopardy if continued. Bad debts were running over 11 percent of sales. This was recognized by management, and I was brought in to rectify the condition.

My first step was to revise and install a methodical collection system. I initiated a reasonable credit policy based on adherence to well defined standards. Both credit approvals and collections were followed strictly according to the systems and policies instituted. My previous bank affiliate experience proved of great value in the process.

Results were immediate as delinquency fell by more than half in a span of 3 to 4 months. At the end of the first year, delinquency was reduced to about 3 percent, and currently it is running between 1 and 2 percent. This percentage is considered exceptional in this type of industry.

Example IV

Treasurer

Forms Two Subsidiary Corporations Effecting a
Nineteen Percent Tax Saving on This Expansion

When my company reached the 52 percent corporate tax bracket, I recommended that a diversification program by means of subsidiary corporations would reduce this figure considerably on future growth and expansion. The board of directors, of which I was a member, agreed to this proposal and I was given go-ahead permission.

After probing into the situation, I proposed the formation of two subsidiary companies. This was accepted by the board and I was instrumental in incorporating a Finance Corporation and a Realty Corporation.

Both of these subsidiaries became highly successful and have accumulated capital in the 33 percent corporate tax bracket. This is a 19 percent saving over what they would have paid as an integral part of the parent organization. In addition, the subsidiaries have been growing substantially, and earnings have been retained by them for their continuing needs for capital growth.

Example V

Sales Manager

Captures Over 59 Percent of Total Canadian Export Sales in His Lines

My company's volume in the Canadian market was out of line compared to estimates and potentials. As Sales Manager, I was requested to take charge of this export business along with my other duties.

I conducted a market research of the entire potential of the sales of these lines in Canada. After studying the situation, I found that representation was insufficient, and in many cases it was very weak. Steps were then taken to strengthen representation by weeding out the poor performers, and by locating additional strong sales-minded companies as representatives. After working up quotas and sales incentives, training sessions were held with representatives and jobber salesmen, which included my accompanying them in field work.

As a direct result of these efforts, the company two years later was doing over 59 percent of all business sold in these lines in Canada.

Example VI

Manager of Manufacturing

Overcomes Bulging Problems on Stainless Steel Production

The addition of stainless steel items manufactured by my company brought a whole new era of problems in bulging. Under the increased pressure needed to bulge stainless steel, the rubber heated up very rapidly and tended to break down after only a few pieces were formed. Trying various methods and types of rubber only created more problems.

Experimenting with a material called urethane, which was used in brake forming, I felt that if it worked in a press brake, it should also work in bulging. After many tests by increasing the clearances and using different lubricants, results became highly satisfactory.

My company is now using urethane as the exclusive medium for bulging on both stainless steel and aluminum. Although double the cost of rubber initially, it outlives rubber by a minimum of a 10 to 1 ratio. In addition, complex shapes which were not considered feasible previously are now in production.

THE RESUME

It is best to prepare the resume first. The "motivation letter" will be easier to write since the essentials can be copied from the resume. Avoid the average resume which reads like a "Job Spec. Sheet." This type contains cold, factual, historical and statistical statements which describe the individual's background, but do not "sell" him. It is sometimes too short, or several closely typed pages too long, and the busy executive will not have time to wade through it. A resume too often lists height, weight, health, religion, etc., which are unimportant factors in securing a career position. A company engages your profit-making capabilities and contributions, and not your "Adonis" appearance.

As the Marketing Manager for a product, you need to dramatize and glamorize your product in a brochure (resume) to create interest. This, now, should be a simple task for you, since you have all of the components required. There is the self-appraisal which includes your educational background, your work history, and the type of person you are. There are the accomplishment stories to prove your capabilities, illustrating not only what you have done, but what you can do for the prospective employer. Combine all of these elements—and you have prepared a "sales" resume.

The best format for a resume consists of an 11″ x 17″ sheet which folds over into a four-page 8 1/2″ x 11″ brochure. The cover page contains your name, address, phone, career image, technical capabilities and personality traits. The inside second page lists some accomplishment stories. The inside third page shows your work history, education and other personal data. If you have a lot of good success stories, use the inside third page also for this purpose. The back cover is then used for your work history, education and personal data. (Refer to the example resumes which follow.)

The cost for the above type of attractive resume brochure may be too expensive to print. If this is so, then use the same 4-page resume, but printed on separate sheets. Be sure that all sheets have your name heading and "page 1 of 1," etc., on each page. Your name on each sheet eliminates the possibility of loss or misplacement when the resume is circulated within the company. Staple all pages together.

Another type of resume is the two single-page approach. It is not as complete as the other formats and should be used only if there are no accomplishments due to lack of experience. This is acceptable for the very young executive or the recent graduate. The first page contains the "career image," traits or characteristics pertinent to a business organization and reason for seeking a position. The second page is composed entirely of personal data. Make certain that your name and address are on both first and second sheets, and that both pages are stapled together to prevent separation in handling. (See example, pages 83 and 84.)

Each success story should have a lead title or heading. The busy executive will not need to read the body copy if the heading tells the story. By the same token, he may take the time to read it entirely if the heading arouses sufficient curiousity.

The best resumes written can never reveal everything about you. Only a personal meeting will accomplish this. The motivation letter whets a company's appetite to learn more about you. *If you enclose the resume with the motivation letter, you greatly reduce your chances for obtaining an interview.*

This is why we strongly recommend that *only in special circumstances* should the resume be enclosed with the motivation letter. If you are in a highly specialized field where only a few companies could be interested in your services, then the resume could be enclosed with the motivation letter. A good example would be the "Sub-Standard/Hard To Place" type of insurance companies of which there are few.

In many instances you will bypass the resume completely in obtaining an interview. However, you have it available should it be needed. Later, under "Interview Techniques," (page 177), the handling of resumes at interviews will be discussed. (Note—A resume sent *before* an interview could very easily screen you *out,* rather than *in.*)

The following section contains examples of resumes based on practically every facet of business or industry. Included are illustrations pertaining to Finance, Sales/Marketing, Manufacturing, Engineering, Administration and Miscellaneous.

MARY A. BRUCE
3911 ROSWELL ROAD N.E.
ATLANTA, GEORGIA 30341
404-522-7717

REGIONAL/DISTRICT SALES MANAGER

EDUCATIONAL MATERIALS

20 Years Record of Success in:

. . . PERSONAL SALES PRODUCTION

. . . RECRUITMENT and TRAINING

. . . SUPERVISION and DIRECTION
of SALES FORCE

A Stable and Mature Decision Maker

Highly Creative

Sales Promotion Oriented

An Excellent Public Speaker with Ability to
Conduct Sales Meetings

Willing to invest talents and skills for long range
career opportunities.

A PLANNER   -   AN ORGANIZER   -   AN IMPLEMENTOR

A FEW ACHIEVEMENTS

INCREASED "POOR" TERRITORY ANNUAL SALES FROM $500,000
TO MORE THAN $2,400,000

The Southeast territory was doing a volume of less than $500,000 when I was assigned to manage the area. Considered a poor volume area by the company, the force consisted only of two sales persons.

I analyzed the area, and decided on a promotional plan to improve the company's image. I recruited, hired and trained competent people and built good will through intensive mailings and personal contacts.

Current sales volume is running better than $2,400,000 annually, with twelve sales people covering the territory. Steadily increasing volume is anticipated and budgeted for.

RESOLVED COMMUNICATION PROBLEM BY PLANNING AND ORGANIZING
NATIONAL SALES MEETINGS

When my company acquired another firm, there existed an ignorance of policies and procedures among the sales people. I was assigned to plan and organize a national sales meeting to acquaint all sales persons with established handlings.

I wrote a 38-page sales manual outlining goals, principles, methods and techniques for the company's specific and unique needs. I planned an agenda, assigning activities to each person based on an assessment of ability to contribute to the meeting through personal participation.

The meeting thoroughly paved the way in resolving the differences arising from the acquisition. Because the sales-force was now better informed, with greater communication facilities, they were happier, and more sales resulted.

PROMOTED SUCCESSFUL CAMPAIGNS TO OBTAIN ADOPTION OF
COMPANY'S TEXTBOOKS

My Company's School Division had been unable to get any books on a certain State's adoption list. Sales volume amounted to approximately $20,000 a year in marginal, non-adoptable materials only.

Through personal contact and special promotional campaigns to that State, I was able to reach a number of persons and describe the value of the content, organization and authorship of the texts. These persons became "advisors" who were convinced of the value of these texts.

As a result, two Social Studies texts were adopted. This raised the volume to over $200,000. Later I was successful in getting several home economics and industrial arts books listed.

BUSINESS HISTORY

SOUTHEAST SALES MANAGER   1971 - Present

Educational Materials
National Publishing Corporation
New York, New York

PSYCHOLOGICAL TESTER   1968 - 1971

Science Research Laboratories
New York, New York

SALES REPRESENTATIVE   1962 - 1968

Textbook Sales
Hanson & Company
New York, New York

REPORTER - FEATURE WRITER   1961 - 1962

Plainsville Morning Herald
Plainsville, South Carolina

EDUCATION

AB (JOURNALISM/EDUCATION)   1961

University of South Carolina

AFFILIATIONS

Journalism Association

Bookmen's Association

PERSONAL

Age-42   Single (Divorced)   Willing to Relocate
                                                       and Travel

-3-

BRUCE R. OSGOOD
315 FOREST AVENUE
MINNEAPOLIS, MINNESOTA 55432
612 - 920-6152

B R A N C H   M A N A G E R

Successfully Dealing With:

MUNICIPAL AND INDUSTRIAL ACCOUNTS

O.E.M. - CONSULTANTS - MAJOR CONTRACTORS

On Highly Sophisticated Equipment

DIESEL AND TURBINE GENERATORS

COMPRESSORS

STEAM CONDENSERS

HIGH PRESSURE BOILER FEED PUMPS

WATER WORKS AND OIL PUMPS

HYDRAULICS - FILTERS

HELICAL AND WORM GEARS

Excellent Communicator - Verbal and Written. Utilizes
Sound Engineering Principles. A Company Team Man
Sales and Profit Oriented

Now Seeking A Career Opportunity Where My Many Skills
and Talents Will Be Utilized To The Fullest Extent For
Higher Management Potential

GOOD ADMINISTRATOR   KNOWLEDGEABLE ENGINEER

TOP-NOTCH SALESMAN

A FEW ACCOMPLISHMENTS

AWARDED $750,000 CONTRACT FOR TURBINE GENERATOR AND BOILER FEED PUMPS BECAUSE OF DESIGN RECOMMENDATIONS

One of my customers, a major paper company, needed a large turbine generator. My company was not considered as a bidder since they had never built a turbine generator of that size, whereas competition had manufactured similar ones previously.

I convinced the paper company that not only could we build the size required, but recommended improvements in design and construction. Working closely with the paper company executives, I showed them that my suggestions would not only improve the performance of the generator, but would require minimal maintenance.

As a direct result of these efforts, my company was awarded a contract not only for the turbine generator, but for the boiler feed pumps as well. The total price was over $750,000. Through six years of operation, the customer is highly impressed by the performance and minimal maintenance which exceeds the proposed guarantees.

OVERCAME LOWER COMPETITIVE BIDS FOR MUNICIPAL MILLION DOLLAR DIESEL GENERATORS

A city in Minnesota was considering the expansion of their power plant for electric power generation, and I contacted the city officials for the bidding on the two units involved.

Meeting after meeting was required to convince the city council and board members that diesel generators would reduce capital costs from $300 per kilowat on a steam plant, to $200 for diesel. Efficiency of a dual fuel (gas and oil) diesel would be 39% vs only 28% on a steam plant. The city finally decided on the purchase of a diesel generator.

Competition was very strong, and our price was the highest. However, I personally contacted every city official and pointed out the merits of my company's design. The ability to change from gas to oil diesel while operating full load without loss of power or frequency, the low plant costs, and the fact that our two units produce 7500 KW firm capacity vs 7000 KW by competition, convinced the city officials to award the contract to us.

My engineering knowledge on the merits of the design and performance of the generators, plus my persistence, resulted in obtaining the contract for over one million dollars!

. . . . . AND MANY MORE SIMILAR ACHIEVEMENTS

BUSINESS HISTORY

BRANCH MANAGER   1967 - Present

Regal Turbine Corporation
Minneapolis, Minnesota

SALES ENGINEER   1963 - 1967

Menlo Pump Company
Chicago, Illinois

MILITARY

PILOT/INSTRUCTOR   1959 - 1963

2nd Lieutenant
U.S. Air Force

EDUCATION

BS - MECHANICAL ENGINEERING   1959

University of Illinois

PROFESSIONAL ASSOCIATIONS

A.S.M.E. Member Grade
Engineers Club of Minneapolis
A.W.W.A Member Committee
Minnesota Municipal Utilities Association
Iowa Association of Municipal Utilities
Member - TAPPI and A.I.S.E.

PERSONAL

Age, 45   Married, 3 children   Willing to relocate
                                               and travel

References on request

-3-

JOHN M. GRIFFIN
6683 WINDY SQUARE
TUCKER, GEORGIA 30151
404-837-4617

S E N I O R   S A L E S M A N

Excellent Growth Potential
To:

ASSISTANT SALES MANAGER

SALES MANAGER

Highly Knowledgeable In:

SEMI-TECHNICAL FIELD OF INDUSTRIAL COMPONENT PRODUCTS

MECHANICAL SYSTEMS OF BUILDING TRADES

Market Familiarity With:

- .. OEM

- .. CONTRACTORS

- .. DISTRIBUTORS

- .. CONSULTANTS

A Top Producer With Administrative Abilities

Strong Personal Motivation And Leadership Qualities

Proven Ability To Work Well With People

NOW SEEKING A GREATER OPPORTUNITY WHERE MY MANY

SKILLS AND TALENTS WILL BE UTILIZED TO THE

FULLEST EXTENT FOR CAREER GROWTH

-1-

A FEW ACCOMPLISHMENTS . . .

SAVED A $140,000 CONTRACT AWARD FOR A CUSTOMER

One of my customers, an insulation contractor, was losing a $140,000
applied insulation order to a competitive bidder and product line.

Calling on the mechanical contractor, who was ready to place the order,
I convinced him of the integrity of his customer, and resold him on our
product.

The insulation contractor not only received the $140,000 contract, but
also was awarded an additional $78,000 contract. This all resulted
through the persuasive efforts I had applied.

SUGGESTION FOR WAREHOUSE OPERATION INCREASED SALES 60%

Finding that we were losing business to competition because they were
able to supply overnight delivery, I suggested a company owned and operated wholesale warehouse to service all insulation contractors.

The company accepted my recommendation and a warehouse was established
to service the entire state.

The first year in operation, my own sales increased over 60% due to pro-
viding better service to a greater number of customers. The company has
since established two more such successful warehouse operations.

- - - - - - - - - - - - - - - -

I was the _first_ salesman in my company to sell the largest consulting
firm in the state on the inclusion of our insulation in their specifications. Three previous salesmen, over a nine year period, were unable
to accomplish this.

- - - - - - - - - - - - - - - -

I was the _first_ salesman in 25 years to sell my territory's Electric
Power Company our insulation products for inclusion in their specifications for their power generating plants. Orders have since been
received for their new units.

- - - - - - - - - - - - - - - -

I sold a $23,000 order for metal building insulation at a price 12%
higher than competitors because of my persistence in explaining the
quality and service of our product. Although I had received management
permission to meet competition, I elected to maintain our price and
profit margin --- and _still got the order_.

-2-

BUSINESS HISTORY

SENIOR SALESMAN   1976 - Present

          Holis Manufacturing Co.
          New York, N.Y.

SALESMAN   1973 - 1976

          Benson Sales Corp.
          Troy, N.Y.

SALES TRAINEE   1972

          Maremont Corporation
          Chicago, Illinois

MILITARY

U.S. NAVY   1966 - 1968

EDUCATION

B.S. BUSINESS ADMINISTRATION   1972

          Emery University
          Decatur, Georgia

PERSONAL

Age - 34   Married, 2 Children   Willing to Relocate
                                                 and Travel

References on request

RAYMOND C. BOLTON
711 BUSSE ROAD
CHICAGO, ILLINOIS 60642
312 - 451-3837

SALES REPRESENTATIVE

With Excellent Potential In Sales Management

to

ASSISTANT SALES MANAGER AND SALES MANAGER

INDUSTRIAL SALES - OEM

TOP CALIBER COMPETENCY - - - -

... An outstanding record of Sales Producing Performance.

... Enthusiasm and creative ability.

... Strong personal motivation.

... Definite leadership and administrative capabilities.

... Proven ability to work well with people.

INCREASED ANNUAL SALES VOLUME FROM $600,000 TO

$2,000,000 in 3 YEARS!

SUCCESSFULLY IMPLEMENTS LONG RANGE SALES GOALS!

CREATIVE   -   PROFIT ORIENTED   -   A SELF-STARTER

HOW SALES INCREASED FROM $600,000 TO OVER $2,000,000 ANNUALLY . . . .

OBTAINS TOTAL BUSINESS FROM FIRM WHICH PREVIOUSLY REFUSED TO DO BUSINESS OR EVEN SEE REPRESENTATIVES FROM COMPANY

I was assigned an account which had refused to do business with my firm. Over the years, a number of our representatives had called on this company and none had been able to obtain an interview, let alone an order.

After repeated calls with no results, I finally obtained an interview with the Director of Purchasing on the basis of an improvement in the design of a metal cap which I had specifically designed for them. Since there was no increase in the cost of the better product, I was able to convince the Director of Purchasing to at least listen to the recommendation.

The new design was accepted and the first order ever received from this company was secured.

- -

On another item used by the same company, I was again told that they would not change suppliers. However, this time I had established an entree and a rapport with them.

I finally convinced the company to change from a molded cap product to a new plastic material with my company making the necessary tooling changes. The chief consideration for the change-over to our product was the technique which I had suggested.

Currently, this firm, in which no salesman could even obtain an interview, is purchasing all their closure supplies from my company. They are now considered a prime account. This firm is so well pleased with both me and my company, that they recently awarded a plaque to us for being an outstanding supplier of theirs.

- - - - SOME MORE ACHIEVEMENTS - - - -

Working persistently with a company, I succeeded in obtaining a new glass container order, but only as a second supplier. In a year and a half, I was able to get 100% of this business. Over $150,000 will be realized this year on this item alone from this company.

- -

I tried to regain lost business from one company, but was unsuccessful until I convinced them that I could improve their quality color standards. Working with the Quality Control and Purchasing Departments, I had my company submit a color standards program which other suppliers would have to match. This resulted in increased volume from $28,000 to over $250,000 annually!

-2-

BUSINESS HISTORY

SALES REPRESENTATIVE

1975 - Present

American Cork Co.
Springfield, Ohio

MILITARY RECORD

U.S. ARMY

STAFF SERGEANT

1969 - 1971

EDUCATION

BBA (MARKETING MAJOR)

1975

University of Wisconsin
Madison, Wisconsin

MEMBERSHIPS

Master Brewers Association of America

Junior Chamber of Commerce

PERSONAL

Age, 32

Married, 3 Children

Willing to Relocate
and Travel

References on Request

HUGH C. GUNDERSON
67 WESTRIDGE DRIVE
MT. PROSPECT, ILLINOIS 60741
312 - 938-2715

<u>SALES/SERVICE ENGINEER</u>

WITH READILY TRANSFERRABLE SKILLS FROM

GLASS PACKAGING TO THE PLASTIC PACKAGING INDUSTRY

INVOLVED IN PRODUCTS FOR . . . .

        ... Food - Beverages
           ... Cosmetics - Pharmaceuticals
            ... Household Chemicals

PROVED SUCCESSFUL METHODS OF . . . .

        ... Increasing Sales
        ... Solving Problems

KNOWLEDGEABLE TECHNICALLY IN . . . .

        ... Liaison between customer, sales and manufacturing departments
          ... Cost and profit oriented for production, sales and service
            ... Plant operations --- new product development

HAS KNOW-HOW TO . . . .
        ... Retain old accounts
        ...Develop and obtain new customers

<u>A SALES AND PROFIT-ORIENTED SELF STARTER</u>

Now Seeking Challenging Opportunity Where My Many Skills And

Abilities Will Be Fully Utilized For Career Growth

-1-

A FEW ACCOMPLISHMENTS

RESOLVED CUSTOMER'S PRODUCTION PROBLEMS - - -
SAVED RETURN OF PRODUCTS WORTH $40,000 - - -

A major manufacturer was encountering production difficulties with glass bottles supplied by my company. This problem could jeopardize an annual volume of over $250,000 purchased by this firm. The immediate problem production run involved the use of 10,000 gross bottles. I was assigned to locate the source of the trouble and correct it. The manufacturer insisted on returning the bottles, which were of private design and therefore would be useless elsewhere.

I investigated the causes of the heavy downtime and discovered that the breakdowns were not due to defective bottles, but to the company's own production problems. They agreed to some changes in their runs which I recommended. The suggestions were carried out while I observed the production. In total, I spent eleven days in their plant.

The manufacturer was very grateful for having their own production problem resolved. The 10,000 gross bottles were not returned, thereby saving my company over $40,000. In addition, the goodwill created resulted in increased purchasing of my company's products.

ELIMINATED COMPETITION THROUGH SPECIAL SERVICE TO CUSTOMER ---

Another supplier and my company shared about equally in the sale of containers to a syrup packing firm. This firm was expanding rapidly and, in the process, was suffering from growing pains with exasperating production problems.

After analyzing the problems, I recommended the use of special types of equipment. I contacted an equipment supplier and worked with them on the necessary machinery to fit the needs of the packing firm, who eagerly accepted the complete layout. In addition, I helped supervise the installation.

Production problems were eliminated and output was increased over 50% in six months. The packing firm showed their appreciation by purchasing all of their containers from my company.

DIRECTED THE SUCCESSFUL INSTALLATION OF A NEW TYPE AUTOMATIC
WASTE TREATMENT SYSTEM ---

When I became a Service Engineer on installations of water and waste treatment equipment, conversion to automatic demineralizers from custom-made units was just taking place. No one, therefore, had actual exper-

-2-

50

105725

ience in the installation of this new type equipment. I was assigned to direct the installation of a completely automatic system costing over $250,000.

Each individual component had to be checked, calibrated and installed properly. It was necessary to coordinate the system in each of its stages. Despite the lack of experience on automatic types, the equipment was so properly installed that it is still on stream after six years of operation. Only routine maintenance is required.

- -

BUSINESS HISTORY

Mansfield Glass Co.   1979 - Present
Mansfield, Ohio
    (Glass and plastic containers)

        Customer service --
        Liaison between customer, manufacturer and sales
           departments. Quality problems, line layout, container
           design and new products.

Industrial Filter and Pump Co.   1970 - 1979
Richmond, Indiana
    (Waste and water treatment equipment)

        Installation and Service

EDUCATION

Loyola University   BA (Chemistry)   1970

ASSOCIATIONS

American Chemical Society
Institute of Food Technologists

PERSONAL

Age - 35   Married, 1 Child   Willing to Relocate
                                       and Travel

References on Request

JANET HOLDEN
3219 S. Emerson Avenue
Dallas, Texas - 76105
(817) - 679-1265

ANCHORWOMAN NEWSCASTER

Action and Results-Oriented TV News Personality

HIGHLY SKILLED AS:

News Director

News Announcer

Investigative Reporter

BASIC EXPERIENCE:

News Reporter

Copywriter

Editor (Tape/Film)

Camerawoman

Film Processor

ASSOCIATED PRESS AWARD:

Best newscast in Texas

ARB RATING:

Highest rated newscast in market area.

CREATIVE - PLANNER - ORGANIZER - INNOVATOR

Well qualified to assume all responsibilities as TV news anchorwoman

52

JANET HOLDEN
3219 S. Emerson Avenue
Dallas, Texas - 76105
(817) - 679-1265

WORK HISTORY

NEWSCASTER   KXAS - TV   1978 - Present
                           Fort Worth-Dallas
                               Texas

NEWS DIRECTOR   KVUE   1976 - 1978
                           Austin, Texas

Started as film processor after graduating college.
Rose through all phases of TV operation to News
Director as listed on first page.

EDUCATION

BBA   Southwestern University   1976

PERSONAL

Age 27   Single   Willing to relocate

References on request

JOSEPH P. JOHNSON
4760 East Palmas Drive
Tucson, Arizona 85710
602 - 298-3405

OFFICE

ASSISTANT

STAFF

with

Eventual Top-Management Potential

Young, Age 25, with some basic experience in:

Purchasing

Accounting

Office Procedures

Production Planning

Expediting

ACTION and RESULT ORIENTED

A persuasive communicator - verbal and written

Outstanding abilities as a

PLANNER   ORGANIZER   IMPLEMENTOR

Now seeking a position in the greater Tucson area with a progressive organization where my abilities can be adapted and utilized to the fullest extent.

54

JOSEPH P. JOHNSON
4760 East Palmas Drive
Tucson, Arizona 85710
602 - 298-3405

BUSINESS HISTORY

Purchasing Agent	Taylor Devices, Inc. 200 Michigan Ave. North Tonawanda, N.Y.	4/79 - Present Left own accord to move to Tucson

Started as bookkeeper and advanced to purchasing agent. Acted as corporate photographer.

Salesman	Hale Office Systems Div. of Remington Rand Cheektowaga, N.Y.	9/78 - 4/79 Left own accord

Photographer	Jean Sardon Studio Deleware Ave. Buffalo, N.Y.	6/78 - 9/78 Left own accord

Many varied positions while attending High School and College, including machine shop work.

EDUCATION

State University of New York	B.A. Political Science	1974 - 1978

Received full New York State Regent's Scholarship.
Total average grade point 3.28 out of a possible 4.0.

INTEREST AREAS

Photography — Film Making — Electronics — Flying

PERSONAL DATA

Age 25 — Married — No Children

References on request

JUDY KIRCHNER
2011 East 6th Avenue
Tucson, Arizona 85733
602 - 786-7324

PERSONNEL MANAGEMENT

Young, age 24, with recently received B.S. Degree in Personnel
Management at the University of Arizona with an earned grade
average of B plus.

Paid for all 4-year school expense by working for Young Women's
Christian Association in numerous capacities including:

Hiring and training of receptionists

Writing procedure manual for front

desk personnel

Various functional duties assigned

Spent one year in work/study program in Israel, working in plastic
factory operating automatic machines to assemble and package
irrigation products for export.

A SYSTEMATIC PLANNER - ORGANIZER - IMPLEMENTOR

A PERSUASIVE COMMUNICATOR - VERBAL & WRITTEN

Now ready to become associated with a progressive, growth-oriented
company where basic needs for challenge and a good career opportunity exist.

JAMES D. BARBOUR
318-8th Avenue West
Minneapolis, Minnesota 55427
612 - 788-6770

SECRETARY-TREASURER

WHOLESALE - RETAIL - MANUFACTURING

CONSUMER PRODUCTS

BROAD, SOUND BACKGROUND IN -

. . . CORPORATE FINANCE

. . . FINANCIAL PLANNING

. . . CREDIT

. . . INSURANCE

. . . TAXES

WITH COROLLARY EXPERIENCE IN -

. . . MERCHANDISING

. . . BUYING

. . . ADVERTISING

. . . WAREHOUSING

WILLING TO INVEST SKILLS AND TALENTS FOR

CAREER OPPORTUNITY IN MORE TEMPERATE CLIMATE

COST CONSCIOUS   -   PROFIT ORIENTED   -   RESULTS MINDED

A FEW ACCOMPLISHMENTS

ESTABLISHES CENTRAL PURCHASING AND WAREHOUSE
RESULTING IN 18% SAVINGS ON LANDED COSTS

Purchasing of merchandise was on a decentralized basis wherein each individual store ordered their own needs. This was done by all 12 stores in the chain. Landed costs were high due to small freight shipments and loss of quantity discounts.

I convinced management to centralize large commodity purchases by establishing a central buying and warehousing installation, and I set up the entire program including the inventory and distribution systems.

Besides a better controlled inventory and a purchasing system, an average 18% was saved on landed costs. It was also possible to now combine promotions on a chain basis rather than the catch-as-catch-can individual store promotion. This resulted in a greater volume sales at reduced advertising expenses.

FORMS TWO SUBSIDIARY CORPORATIONS EFFECTING A 19%
TAX SAVING ON THE EXPANSION

When my company reached the 52% corporate tax bracket, I recommended that a diversification program by means of subsidiary corporations would reduce this figure considerably on future growth and expansion. The Board of Directors, of which I was a member, agreed to this proposal and I was given the go-ahead permission.

After probing into the situation, I proposed the formation of two subsidiary companies. This was accepted by the Board and I was instrumental in incorporating a Finance Corporation and a Realty Corporation.

Both of these subsidiary corporations became highly successful and have accumulated capital in the 33% corporate tax bracket. This is a 19% saving over what they would have paid as an integral part of the parent organization. In addition, the subsidiaries have been growing substantially, and earnings have been retained by them for their continuing needs for capital growth.

INCREASES SHARE VALUE BY "PLOWING BACK" EARNINGS
VERSUS PAYING CASH DIVIDENDS

It was the practice of my company to pay out 100% of earnings on stock each year. This practice tended to restrict growth, cut down on needed working capital and subjected the many stockholders to needless taxes when using cash dividends to purchase additional stock.

A study was made by me on the effects of "plowing back" corporate earnings for the benefits gained thereby to individual stock holders. The study revealed that a 24% gain in after tax net worth would have been effected over the 5 year period reviewed

The Directors, with the stockholders approval, voted for this method. For the past seven years, stockholders have received substantial tax savings plus earnings on a compound interest basis. Share value increased by the amount of annual per share earnings. In 1967, a 100% stock dividend was declared because of the increased share value.

-2-

BUSINESS HISTORY

SECRETARY-TREASURER   1960 - Present

R & R COMPANY
AND   Minneapolis, Minnesota

MEMBER OF THE BOARD   12 Retail Stores
                      Hardware-Furniture-Lumber Chain

                      R & R Wholesale and Warehouse
                      R & R Trucking Company
                      Northern Finance Corporation
                      Northern Realty Corporation

EDUCATION

UNIVERSITY OF MINNESOTA   BBA   1960

Various other business and management courses

MILITARY RECORD

U.S. Air Force   1953 - 1956

1st Lieutenant
Combat Fighter Pilot
"Flying Tigers"

PERSONAL DATA

Age 48   Married - 4 Children   Willing to Relocate

Private and Commercial Pilot's License

References on Request

FREDERICK E. POTTER
717 EAST CARLISLE AVENUE
LAKE FOREST, ILLINOIS
312 - 424-2563

CORPORATE ACCOUNTING EXECUTIVE

With Extensive Background In:

* PREPARING AND ANALYZING MONTHLY FINANCIAL STATEMENTS

* ESTIMATING MONTHLY INVENTORIES

* HANDLING COMPANY INSURANCE AND WORKMEN'S COMPENSATION PLAN

* BUDGET PREPARATION AND CONTROL

* FEDERAL AND STATE TAXES

* COST ACCOUNTING PRACTICES

* PRICING OF OVER 10,000 ITEMS

Dependable, Competent Decision Maker With
Excellent Record Of Accomplishments. Well
Qualified To Assume Corporate Accounting
Responsibilities With Progressive Manu-
facturing Company

. . . . . . A FEW ACCOMPLISHMENTS

ORIGINATED COMPARATIVE MONTHLY BREAKDOWN REPORT
INDICATING LOSS OR GAIN

As Assistant Treasurer, I discovered that Profit and Loss Statements were prepared on a cumulative basis derived from general posting rather than by component breakdowns by month. To overcome this oversight, I devised a form which
detailed each element and factor composing all the shipments and manufacturing
expenses of the company by month.

This comparative statistical breakdown indicated at a glance where weaknesses
could be immediately corrected to increase the profit structure. It became a
valuable guide to both the Sales Vice President and the Operating Vice President as to the strong and weak points of their operations.

PROVED REPAIR ENTRIES ON TAX RETURNS AND AVOIDED
ADDITIONAL 52% ASSESSMENTS

In 1976 and 1977 the Internal Revenue Department proposed to disallow $60,000
and $80,000 respectively for repairs deducted from the tax returns which I had
helped to prepare. They claimed these to be Capital Expenditures which should
be set up as Capital items and depreciated over a period of 15 to 20 years.

I personally conducted the Internal Revenue Agent through the plant and proved
to the Agent's satisfaction that these items should be considered in the nature
of repairs.

By allowing the repair entries on the tax returns, the company was not assessed
additional taxes in the amount of 52% of the $60,000 and $80,000 which they
would have had to pay were they treated as Capital Expenditures.

REWORKED COST FIGURES WHICH HELPED TO INCREASE BOTH
SALES AND PROFITS

When I first assumed the position of Chief Cost Accountant, the firm had no
cost accounting system on "specials". Also very little attention was paid to
standard cost accounting since the profit picture showed a good gain.

I reworked the entire cost figures, wrote a complete cost manual and priced the
"special" items based on the revised cost figures.

As a result, the company became more competitive on bidding for jobs, and was
thus able to materially increase its sales. The continuous application of cost
principles was a definite factor in the company's progress over the years both
in sales volume and net profits.

-2-

BUSINESS HISTORY

ASSISTANT TREASURER   1968 - Present

Waukegan Screw Products Co.
Waukegan, Illinois

SENIOR ACCOUNTANT   1955 - 1968

Steinberg & Steinberg
Certified Public Accountants

MILITARY RECORD

U.S. ARMY   1951 - 1955

Captain
Finance Corps

EDUCATION

B.S. (ACCOUNTING & ECONOMICS)   1951

University of Wisconsin

Numerous financial and other courses including Data Processing

ASSOCIATION MEMBERSHIPS

National Association of Accountants

PERSONAL DATA

Age - 53   Married - No Children   Willing to Relocate

References on Request

LEONARD J. WARDMAN
1759 UPTON AVENUE
SPARTANSBURG, SOUTH CAROLINA 29303
803 - 274-1978

CONTROLLER

Analytical ability to determine the facts

Adaptable to new ideas to achieve objectives

Skilled at motivating people

Effectively operates in relationship to production,
marketing, engineering and research and development.

A TEAM WORKER

Experienced:

Management Reports....Cost Accounting....Financial Analysis

Executive Development....EDP....Systems and Procedures

Taxes....Forecasting and Planning....Budgets....Insurance

Evaluation and Supervision of Personnel...Procurement

General Office Management

Acquisitions

-1-

NEW CONCEPT - NEW POSITION

A multi-plant and multi-division concept was inefficient, and management decided upon a centrally controlled department to which I was assigned to direct the accounting operation. I developed a concept and accounting philosophy built around centralized control data processing, established accounting policies and procedures and trained the necessary personnel to effectively operate this program. The program was completed, which previously had included fifty separate locations, and resulted in a 40% reduction of personnel cost, and further provided one policy and method for evaluation of inventories and was consistent in the handling of intra-company business. This led to more efficient operation, more meaningful information for management, and cost information on a comparable basis throughout the company.

NEW ACQUISITION PROGRAM

A new acquisition ($70 million) was acquired by the parent company. I was assigned as the only man from the parent company, as chief finance officer, to bring this acquisition into the parent organization. I changed the accounting procedure, financial control and operations, into parent company policies. All phases of changes in operation were successfully integrated with no lapse in activity, in manufacturing, sales, accounting and overall operations. This allowed management to do a more efficient job in controlling costs and resulted in an annual savings of $100,000. In addition, there was a 20% increase in sales volume, while reducing accounting personnel by 10%.

COMPUTER UTILIZATION

The information available to management required too long to obtain, the costs were too high, and the information was not of much value. Recognizing the operation capacity of an available computer, I designed and developed a concept to achieve the data required, by working with data processing personnel and directing the program. The information obtained provided a sales and profit forecast on specific products that was more meaningful to management. In addition, the information was utilized weekly for the basis of decisions on merchandising. Management was able to do more effective planning which resulted in increased sales for the company.

INSTALLATION OF DIRECT COST SYSTEM

Management had made the decision to change from an antiquated actual cost system to a modern standard cost system, using the direct cost philosophy. I was assigned the responsibility of supervising this change in policy. I completely reorganized the cost accounting department in all interacting relationships with other operating departments, and implemented the direct cost program. Results of this program provided data to management for better direction of company policies. More effective and efficient cost control resulted in better sales-planning and profit-planning by product.

BUSINESS HISTORY

SOUTHERN TEXTILES CORPORATION   1977 - Present

Spartanburg, South Carolina

        Management Information Center   — 1 year

        Manager Cost and Inventory
        Accounting Department

        Controller   — 2 years

        Assistant Controller   — 1 year

        Assistant Manager Cost Department   — 1 Year

UNITED MILLS CORPORATION

Asheville, North Carolina   1967 - 1977

        Assistant Corporate Controller

GENERAL ELECTRIC COMPANY   1963 - 1967

Bridgeport, Connecticut

        Accountant

EDUCATION

B.S. ACCOUNTING & FINANCE   1962

        University of North Carolina

AFFILIATIONS

National Association of Accountants

PERSONAL DATA

Age - 40   Married - 2 Children   Willing to Relocate

References on Request

HERBERT M. VALLOR
214 WEST MARION STREET
MUSKEGON, MICHIGAN 49441
616 - 744-4297

C O N T R O L L E R

C H I E F   C O S T   A C C O U N T A N T

A Systematic Planner And Organizer With

Solid Background And Heavy Experience In:

BUDGET AND EXPENSE CONTROL

NEW PRODUCT DEVELOPMENT EVALUATION

REPORTING SYSTEMS

INVENTORY ROUTINES

PRODUCT COST DETERMINATION

MANUFACTURING OVERHEAD

GENERAL COST REDUCTION APPROACHES

INVENTORY REVALUATIONS

PHYSICAL INVENTORY

EVALUATION OF PLANT INVESTMENTS

COST DISTRIBUTION

CONSTRUCTION AUDITING

MANUFACTURING LOSS REPORTING

....OUTSTANDING RECORD OF ACHIEVEMENTS

IN COST REDUCTION....

DEVELOPS SYSTEM TO POINT OUT SUB-STANDARD PROFITABILITIES

My company has a broad range of products manufactured in approximately 35 different direct labor manufacturing units. However, it has been a practice to apply a single standard manufacturing overhead rate to each direct labor dollar in determining product costs used to arrive at profit contribution by product.

Realizing the inaccuracies of this method, I developed a system wherein each indirect manufacturing cost was accumulated as it applied to each of the direct labor units.

With this information, it is now possible to calculate a much more sensitive indirect overhead rate for each manufacturing unit. Applying these differentiated rates, the resultant product cost affords a much more accurate profit determination, thus pointing out products with sub-standard profitability that had been disguised by the standard single overhead adder.

DEVISES "BUSINESS ANALYSIS" METHOD TO RANK

PROPOSED DEVELOPMENTS OF NEW PRODUCTS

An accelerated engineering program on new product development was just initiated when I was assigned to the department. Not having any previous need for an evaluation system, the department was ill-equipped to handle the expansion.

I developed a method of correlating all the information needed to select, measure and control product development expenditures. It was necessary to rank the proposed projects from a profit standpoint to provide a sound business basis in selecting those programs on which the department could most profitably spend its resources.

The "Business Analysis" which I instituted for each project enabled the company to undertake about 30 programs out of 70 to 80 proposed, thereby eliminating unnecessary expenditures with resultant savings in money and time.

MAJOR FUNCTIONS IN PRESENT POSITION

Analysis of new product introduction opportunities.
Manufacturing expense reporting.
Engineering expense reporting.
Preparation of manufacturing and engineering budgets.
Inventory revaluations.
Evaluation of plant investments.
Supervision.

-2-

BUSINESS HISTORY

SUPERVISOR – EXPENSE CONTROL   1968 – Present

Spencer Electric Company
Manufacturing & Engineering Divisions
Muskegon, Michigan

EDUCATION

B.S. BUSINESS ADMINISTRATION   1968

Syracuse University

PERSONAL DATA

Age – 37   Married – 2 Children   Willing to Relocate

References on Request

LEONARD M. MURRELL
12461 Livermore Avenue
Detroit, Michigan 48227
313 - 786-8061

FINANCIAL/COST ANALYST

Broad Experience In:

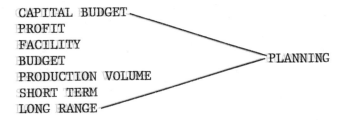

CAPITAL BUDGET
PROFIT
FACILITY
BUDGET   PLANNING
PRODUCTION VOLUME
SHORT TERM
LONG RANGE

Ability To Write And Present Management Programs Based on
Costs, Budgets and Profits.

Background in Industrial Management/Engineering And, As
Consultant, Affords Firsthand Knowledge of
Plant Operations.

Performed Studies And Analysis On Acquisitions, Improvements,
Investments And Plant Relocations.

Familiar With Data Processing, Systems And Procedures.

A FEW ACCOMPLISHMENTS . . . . . .

REDUCES SCRAP COSTS OVER 70% IN EIGHT MONTHS

Defective material and defective work in metal working and assembling departments were running very high and unprofitable percentages existed when I was assigned the task to reduce and minimize these costly expenditures.

I discovered that routine reports were created at irregular intervals and scrap was frequently removed to the metal scrap areas by the production departments without the knowledge of the inspection department.

Instituting an educational campaign describing the objectives with both departments, I devised a weekly reporting system which defined the sources causing the underlying problems. Once known, they could be attacked and corrected.

As a direct result, over an eight month period, Labor, Material and Burden defect costs were reduced 62% in the Press Room, 95% in the Metal Sub-Assembly Department, and 63% in the Metal and Body Assembly Department.

RECOMMENDATION REDUCES CAPITAL FUND APPROPRIATION BY 33%

Actual requests for capital funds for tooling and production facilities were substantially in excess of original corporate cost and capital expenditure estimates.

I analyzed the project and planning for both tooling and production, and reviewed recently removed equipment. Holding meetings with manufacturing management, plant engineering and finance personnel, I pointed out the use of recently removed equipment which could be modified and utilized.

These recommendations were accepted and requests for capital funds for these projects were reduced to below the original corporate cost estimates. The reduction in actual funds appropriation amounted to over 33% without sacrificing efficiency and production capacity.

ANALYZES FOREIGN MARKET EXPANSION AND
RECOMMENDS INVESTMENT APPROPRIATION

My company approved a 1-million dollar capital appropriation request as a start towards expanding foreign sales operations in order to increase domestic production and, thereby, increase domestic profits.

As Financial and Investment Analyst on the corporate staff, I analyzed the foreign market sales volume in units and dollars, and similar volumes of competitive companies and its effect on capital and profit.

My findings were accepted and foreign operations proved to be profitable. A year later the corporation conducted further investment analysis with the result that 40 million dollars more were invested. In spite of the original organizational costs, a 1% profit was realized the first year of operation.

-2-

BUSINESS HISTORY

FINANCIAL ANALYST   1973 - Present
             Alben Profit Planning, Inc.
                  Detroit, Michigan

COST ANALYST   1966 - 1973
                  American Motors
                Milwaukee, Wisconsin

COST ANALYST   1961 - 1966
             Packard Manufacturing Co.
                   Toledo, Ohio

STAFF INDUSTRIAL ENGINEER   1958 - 1961
             Industrial Products Planning
             Industrial Controls Division
           Westinghouse Air Brake Company
               Pittsburgh, Pennsylvania

EDUCATION

B.S. INDUSTRIAL ENGINEERING   1958
                University of Wisconsin

PRODUCTION ENGINEERING
                 Marquette University
                 (Evening Courses)

Various Specialized Company Courses

ASSOCIATION MEMBERSHIPS

           National Association of Accountants
           Industrial Management Society
           American Institute of Management
           American Materials Handling Society

PERSONAL DATA

Age - 47   Single   Willing to Relocate
                                                   and Travel

References on Request

LEWIS MANTER
c/o Mother
ROSE MANTER
6821 E. Speedway
Tucson, Arizona 85712
602 - 364-8281

SENIOR STAFF ASSISTANT
to a
PRESIDENT or SENIOR EXECUTIVE

FULLY KNOWLEDGEABLE

with DIVERSIFIED EXPERIENCE

and PROVEN ABILITY

in all phases of:

Computer Control

Systems Analysis

Logistics

Liaison

Technical Services

Property Administration

Material Maintenance

Inventory Control

Warehousing

Personnel

Training

A PROBLEM SOLVER - An ORGANIZER - An IMPLEMENTOR
and
PROFIT ORIENTED

Presently working in Africa, but now seeking a
corporate position in the United States with a
progressive organization where my many skills
and abilities will be fully utilized for career
growth.

c/o Mother
ROSE MANTER
6821 E. Speedway
Tucson, Arizona 85712
602 - 364-8281

BUSINESS HISTORY

SENIOR COMPUTER CONTROL SUPERVISOR	Morrison-Knudson Co., Inc. Zaire, Africa	1980 - Present
MANAGER, MAINTENANCE and LOGISTICS DEPARTMENTS	Pacific Architects & Engineers Okinawa	1971 - 1980
SALESMANAGER	Turin Motors Okinawa	1970 - 1971

MILITARY RECORD

CARTOGRAPHER	U.S. Air Force California & Okinawa	1966 - 1970

EDUCATION

Business Management	Indiana University	1966
College Preparatory	Graduate	1965
U.S. Army Map Compiling Course	Fort Belvoir, Virginia	

Various other courses to further my education including Business Administration courses at the University of Southern California which were paid for by the U.S. Air Force.

PERSONAL DATA

Age - 36	Married - 2 children	Willing to relocate and travel

References on request

LENORA H. JOYCE
814 Sherman Avenue
Anoka, Minnesota 55467
612 - 274-9128

O F F I C E   M A N A G E R

C H I E F   A C C O U N T A N T

MANUFACTURING - DISTRIBUTORS - WHOLESALE

COMPETENT ADMINISTRATOR EXPERIENCED

IN

MANAGEMENT PRINCIPLES AND PRACTICES

BACKGROUND IN -

        ... OFFICE MANAGEMENT

        ... GENERAL ACCOUNTING

        ... CREDIT AND COLLECTIONS

        ... PURCHASING

KNOWLEDGEABLE IN -

        ... FINANCE

        ... TRAFFIC

        ... INSURANCE

        ... TAXES

        ... LEASES

A GOOD SYSTEM ANALYST: WRITING - REVISING -

AND INSTALLING PROCEDURES

-1-

A FEW ACCOMPLISHMENTS . . .

REORGANIZES INEFFECTIVE DEPARTMENT INTO SMOOTH RUNNING OPERATION

When I became Office Manager, I found work functions were running as much as two to three months behind on billings and financial statements. Daily financial, sales and comparative analysis reports were unavailable. Accounts were inaccurate since payments were made in error due to uncertainty of terms by dealers. Aging and collection follow-ups were in a deplorable condition. Necessary management decisions were therefore delayed.

After studying the work loads, I reorganized the entire department. I streamlined the work flow and created shortcuts by devising and installing forms and form letters to speed up and systematize all functions.

As a result, all bottlenecks were eliminated, daily financial and sales reports were issued on time, and credit and collection functions became accurate and current. Management was thus able to review operations on a daily basis and make decisions accordingly.

EFFECTS SAVING IN INVENTORY LOSS THROUGH BETTER SYSTEM

I found a field inventory of demonstration machines amounting to over $120,000 which were memoed and with virtually no control over them. Some of the equipment was even unpriced. Because of the loose memo handling, it could not be determined whether the merchandise was in the possession of the salesmen, dealers or the distributors. In the transfer process many of the machines were eventually lost since salesmen were lax in supplying transfer memos.

I initiated a system wherein all merchandise was billed to salesmen at regular prices and for which they were personally responsible. When goods were sold or transferred, the salesman filled out a form which was sent to the credit department for approval. This form was the basis for rebilling to the proper account. Once a month the salesman received a copy of all transactions by him, which he had to verify, sign and return to the company.

Every item of demonstration merchandise was thus accountable for and shown at actual dollar value at all times. A considerable saving in inventory loss was thereby effected, as well as a reduction in clerical handling time.

MORE EFFICIENT HANDLINGS AND CONTROL RESULT IN BETTER CUSTOMER RELATIONS

There was no definite control on orders after entering the plant for production in connection with the billing department. The proper paperwork was not received for billing purposes which resulted in many shipped items being unaccounted for.

I installed a check system with the production office to establish an absolute control on machines shipped and billed. By initiating a change in the company's original entry of orders, a complete cycle of control was established.

Specific responsibilities were pinpointed in each area thereby eliminating the existing condition. Greater efficiency, good customer relations and good will were gained as a direct result of these corrective measures.

BUSINESS HISTORY

OFFICE MANAGER   1976 – Present

            Sampson Manufacturing Company
                Minneapolis, Minnesota

ASSISTANT CONTROLLER   1972 – 1976
CREDIT MANAGER
            Anoka, Manufacturing Company
                Anoka, Minnesota

ACCOUNTANT   1971 – 1972

            Central Credit Corporation
                Minneapolis, Minnesota

ACCOUNTANT   1970 – 1971

              Pure Oil Company
              Minneapolis, Minnesota

EDUCATION

DAKOTA BUSINESS COLLEGE   Graduate – December 1969

OTHER COURSES:-

      INTERSTATE BUSINESS COLLEGE

      DUN & BRADSTREET CREDIT AND FINANCIAL ANALYSIS

      INTERNATIONAL ACCOUNTANTS SOCIETY COURSES

PERSONAL DATA

Age – 33   Single   Willing to Relocate

References on Request

VICTOR E. STEFFES
737 Sunnyside Avenue
Memphis, Tennessee 38126
901 - 822-5817

OFFICE MANAGER/STAFF ADMINISTRATOR

Ten Year Background In -

MANAGEMENT, ADMINISTRATION, PURCHASING, and other SUPERVISORY POSITIONS

BROADLY EXPERIENCED IN:

....Organizing - Coordinating - Motivating

....Office Procedures, Methods, and Machines

....Purchasing, Procurement Procedures and Resources

....Record Maintenance - Micro-film Systems and Equipment

THOROUGHLY FAMILIAR WITH:

....Basic Accounting

....Processing of Funds - Receipt and Disbursal

....Inventory and Cost Control

....Customer Relations

....Personnel

AN ORGANIZER OF EFFICIENT AND EFFECTIVE BUSINESS OPERATIONS

WITH KNOWLEDGE OF DATA PROCESSING APPLICATIONS

-1-

A FEW ACCOMPLISHMENTS . . . . .

INSTITUTED INVENTORY CONTROL SYSTEM RESULTING IN IMMEDIATE COST SAVINGS

When assigned the duty of Purchasing Agent, I soon found there was no firm policy or adequate system in operation. This resulted in over-payments, out-of-stock, stoppages and waste conditions.

I immediately instituted a system for inventory control, stock coding and storage evaluation. Standardization and application of efficient purchasing procedures were established.

This resulted in immediate savings, heavy cost reduction and functional efficiency, continuing more effectively each year.

RECOMMENDED MICRO-FILMING THEREBY REDUCING VALUABLE SPACE PROBLEM

Records requiring micro-filming were contracted to an outside source. My evaluation studies indicated that internal operation of this function could result in considerable savings, primarily due to ever increasing volume of these records.

Acting on my recommendations, essential equipment was purchased and put into operation. Immediate results were a reduction in labor, elimination of 80% of necessary file space, and more immediate internal information. Also, due to the increased volume of records, the savings amounted to approximately $60,000 annually.

WHAT OTHERS SAY . . . . .

"....In my estimation, Mr. Steffes rates 'excellent' in both ability and management qualifications. I have known him almost ten years and he has continually proven his ability. . ."

A Former Superior

".....It was my good fortune to have worked with Victor Steffes as Officers of the Purchasing Agents Association of Tennessee. During this five year period, Victor demonstrated his ability to manage well the affairs of our organization and encourage people to get the job done . . . ."

Vice-President, Purchasing
Steel Fabricating Company

-2-

BUSINESS HISTORY

COMPANY SECRETARY   1974 - Present

PURCHASING AGENT

Hospital Association of Tennessee, Inc.
Memphis, Tennessee

QULAITY CONTROL   1973 - 1974
TEST ANALYST

Alabama Coal & Iron Company
Fairmont, Alabama

MILITARY RECORD

U.S. AIR FORCE   1971 - 1973

1st Lieutenant
Salvage Officer

EDUCATION

UNIVERSITY OF GEORGIA   B.S. CHEMISTRY   1970

Other courses:
   Business Adminstration, Economics, Accounting and Management

AFFILIATIONS

American Chemical Society

National Association of Purchasing Agents

PERSONAL DATA

Age - 32   Married - 2 Children   Willing to Relocate
                                                       and Travel

References on Request

JOHN R. KRUEGER
7028 Clair Court
Kewaskum, Wisconsin 53214
414 - 332-6814

O F F I C E   M A N A G E R

Competent Administrator Experienced
In
Management Principles And Practices

* * * * * *

Broad Knowledge And Background In:

ADMINISTRATION

SYSTEMS AND PROCEDURES

IN-PLANT PRINTING

OFFICE SERVICES

PERSONNEL

FORMS CONTROL (DESIGN & PURCHASE)

TRAINING

SALES

* * * * * *

As Senior Systems Analyst, Wrote,
Revised And Installed Procedures

Capable Of Comprehending Technical
Data

Functions Well Under Pressure

CREATIVE ABILITY   —   GOOD ORGANIZER   —   AN IMPLEMENTOR

80

.......A FEW ACCOMPLISHMENTS

DEVISED A SYSTEM WHICH SAVED OVER $7,000 ANNUALLY

As Office Manager, I assumed the task to formulate a procedure to handle closed orders in the Cost Department. These costs were hand posted and accumulated until a job was completed. The hand-posting was a laborious and time consuming operation.

Analyzing the situation, I developed a procedure in which all the costs were key punched and controlled by an open and closed file in the Data Processing Department.

Since this method required only one key punch operator and a small additional Data Processing machine, it eliminated the functions of five clerks.

The cost of the machine and the punch operator's time amounted to $400 monthly. The reduction of the five clerk's salaries were better than $1,000 per month. This left a net saving of about $600 per month or $7,200 per year using my system. In addition, the costing was more accurate with a faster report in the hands of management.

REORGANIZED AND REVITALIZED ENTIRE DEPARTMENT

After assuming the position of Office Manager, I found that there had been no coordination of work, and operations were in a turmoil with much duplication of work and effort.

Filing time was about six weeks behind and there were just stacks of papers lying in piles. No rules or regulations had been established for mail handling, with the result that time consuming duplication of effort existed.

My first step was to re-organize the entire operational set up in the department. I instituted a Central File-Mail operation and trained the supervisor in work measurement, better filing methods and mail handling. I wrote a Mail Processing Manual and installed a new alpha-numerical filing system to replace the antiquated alphabetical method in use. Then I designed and had new mailing racks built and set up a scheduled mail delivery for all departments in the plant.

In addition to a smooth flowing, on-time operation, this re-organization of the department caused the elimination of 2 employees resulting in a $5,000 annual saving.

..................AND MANY MORE SIMILAR ACCOMPLISHMENTS!..................

BUSINESS HISTORY

OFFICE MANAGER AND
SENIOR SYSTEMS ANALYST

1974 - Present

Stanford Manufacturing Co.
Milwaukee, Wisconsin

SALESMAN

1972 - 1974

Johnson Calculating Service, Inc.
Milwaukee, Wisconsin

OFFICE MANAGER

1969 - 1972

Martin Service Company
Milwaukee, Wisconsin

EXECUTIVE ASSISTANT

1968 - 1969

Associated Hospital Services
Milwaukee, Wisconsin

EDUCATION

BBA - INDUSTRIAL MANAGEMENT

1968

University of Wisconsin

PROFESSIONAL AFFILIATIONS

Systems and Procedures Association
Administration Management Society
In-Plant Printing Association

PERSONAL DATA

Age - 37   Married - 1 Child   Willing to Relocate

References on Request

JAMES R. LINDBERG
1439 Wilson Boulevard
Arlington, Virginia 22205
703 - 527-2643

<u>ADMINISTRATIVE ASSISTANT</u>

with

<u>EVENTUAL TOP-MANAGEMENT POTENTIAL</u>

YOUNG, AGE 28, WITH DEGREES IN LAW AND ENGINEERING

ACTION - AND - RESULT ORIENTED

A persuasive communicator, verbal and written

creative---imaginative---versatile

Outstanding abilities as a:

PLANNER

ORGANIZER

IMPLEMENTOR

Now Seeking A Career With A Progressive Organization Where My Educational Background And Administrative Abilities Can Be Adapted And Utilized
To The Fullest Extent For Future Growth.

-1-

83

JAMES R. LINDBERG
1439 Wilson Boulevard
Arlington, Virginia 22205
703 - 527-2643

BUSINESS HISTORY

PATENT EXAMINER	U.S. Patent Office Washington, D.C.	1977 - Present
JUNIOR ENGINEER	Maryland Electric Power Co. Baltimore, Maryland	1975 - 1977
SUMMER JOBS	Working in Boatyard and Electromechanical Assembly Plants	

EDUCATION

UNIVERSITY OF VIRGINIA	BS Mechanical Engineering	1973
AMERICAN UNIVERSITY	Juris Doctor	1979

MILITARY RECORD

U.S. NAVY	Lt. j.g.	1973 - 1975

MEMBERSHIPS

American Society of Mechanical Engineers
Maryland Bar Association
Maryland Boat Club

INTEREST AREAS

MARINE PRODUCTS:
Shipbuilding--Engines--Boats Of All Types

PERSONAL DATA

Age 28	Married	Willing to Relocate

REFERENCES ON REQUEST

-2-

84

MARION L. MULLEN
2650 LAKE SHORE DRIVE
CHICAGO, ILLINOIS 60612
312 - 241-5722

T O P   E C H E L O N   E X E C U T I V E

IN

CONSUMER LOAN & SALES FINANCE

Currently Divisional Vice President With Two Area Vice Presidents
Reporting To Me, And A Total Of Over 1,000 Personnel

Responsibilities Included Operation Of Over 200 Branches And Several
Industrial Banks Throughout United States And Canada With Continuing
Profitable Investment Of Funds Totalling Approximately 250 Million Dollars.

Fully Knowledgeable In All Functions Including:

ACQUISITIONS	---	COLLECTIONS
PROMOTIONS	---	BUDGETING
FORECASTING	---	AUDITING

COMMERCIAL REAL ESTATE

PERSONNEL TRAINING AND DEVELOPMENT

* * * * * * *

COMBINED EXPERIENCE UNEQUALLED IN LOAN AND SALES FINANCE BUSINESS

* * * * * * *

AN INNOVATOR   A PROBLEM SOLVER   A DECISION MAKER

AND

A PROFIT-ORIENTED EXECUTIVE

-1-

A FEW CAPABILITIES

Able To Integrate Both Personal Loan And Sales Finance Operations
Avoiding Pitfalls In The Process.

* * * * *

Actively Involved In Acquisitions Of Other Companies
And
Directly Responsible For Integration Of Large Groups Of Personnel.

* * * * *

Skilled In Surveying, Negotiating Leases, Expansion Into New Areas.
And Preparation And Attainment Of Yearly Profit Plan.

* * * * *

Knowledgeable In The Conversion To Data Processing
And
Can Help Resolve Field Problems Connected With Installation Of System.

* * * * *

Understands Credit And Casualty Insurance As They
Relate To The Loan And Sales Finance Business

* * * * *

An Administrator Who Surrounds Himself With Capable
People And Obtains Maximum Performance.

* * * * *

A Fluent Writer And Speaker And Conductor Of
Inspiring Meetings And Technical Seminars.

* * * * *

Has Talents Valuable To The Right Company And Can
Quickly Demonstrate Ability To Make Money For Them.

-2-

. . . . . .SOME ACCOMPLISHMENTS

BUILT NEW CANADIAN BRANCHES INTO HIGHLY PROFITABLE OPERATION

One of my assignments was to open up a Canadian operation. Since there was no previous history, it was necessary to establish a credit policy that was competitive, but one which would not produce losses and expenses beyond the ability to make a profit.

Conditions as to quality of customer, amount and value of collateral, and income of customer were substantially different from those in the United States. It took six months of investigation, analysis and actual experience before a credit policy could be firmed up which would have an edge on competition and yet make for a profitable operation.

An additional problem had to be resolved in acquiring and indoctrinating new personnel for the branches opened. After attracting a few experienced personnel from competition, most of the balance of personnel came personally as referrals from men already hired. Supervisory personnel from my United States operations provided the training and indoctrination.

The Canadian operation became one of the most successful and profitable operations in the Company. Over a five year period, I opened 37 branches and built up 27 million dollars in outstanding receivables with an operating income of approximately 2½ million dollars.

REVITALIZED POOREST TERRITORY INTO MOST PROFITABLE WITH GREATEST EXPANSION

The Company was seriously considering selling a territory where delinquency was high, losses were higher, volume was down and profits were practically nil. As a last resort, the Company asked me to take charge and see what could be done to revitalize the territory and re-establish it on a profitable basis.

I first determined which District Managers and Managers were capable with proper training to do the kind of job to be successful. Gaining control of losses and expenses, upgrading the quantity and quality of the volume and improving the quality of personnel, took about a year and a half. Meanwhile I recruited other qualified personnel and was soon expanding the number of branches.

During a five year period, the number of branches were more than tripled. From the poorest territory in the Company, it became the one showing the highest profits on investment. It had the lowest employee turnover, lowest losses, lowest delinquency and showed the best growth.

As a result of this outstanding performance, I was promoted to Vice President!

BUSINESS HISTORY

VICE PRESIDENT/DIVISION MANAGER   1961 – Present

Hobart Finance Corporation
Chicago, Illinois

MANAGER   1957 – 1961

Universal Management Corporation
Newark, Ohio

EDUCATION

B.S. FINANCE – BANKING   1953

Wharton School of Finance

MASTERS DEGREE – BUSINESS ADMINISTRATION   1956

Harvard University

PROFESSIONAL AFFILIATIONS

Illinois Association Of Consumer Finance

Board Of Directors In Consumer Finance Trade Associations
In States Of:

Illinois
Pennsylvania
New York

PERSONAL DATA

Age – 52   Married – 4 Children   Willing to Relocate
and Travel

REFERENCES ON REQUEST

FREDERICK J. HALL
4822 Connecticut Avenue N.W.
Washington, D.C. 20045

ATTORNEY

With Long-range Potential As -

SECRETARY and/or TREASURER

Young, age 33, with degrees in Law and Mechanical Engineering.
Competent in estimating situations, gathering and evaluating
information and presenting facts in a logical, articulate and
professional manner.

INVOLVED IN:

        ...Profit Sharing Plans
        ...Investments and Trusts
        ...Anti-Trust and Unfair Trade Practices
        ...Patent Litigation
        ...Patent Licensing, Domestic and Foreign
        ...Management Information Sciences (Data Processing)

EXPERIENCED AS:

        ...Private Attorney (General Law Practice)
        ...Patent Attorney (Corporate)
        ...Patent Examiner (U. S. Patent Office)
        ...Product Engineer
            (Power equipment, engines, sleeve bearings,
            aluminum forging, nylon production.)

A SYSTEMATIC PLANNER _____ ORGANIZER _____ IMPLEMENTOR

        A PERSUASIVE COMMUNICATOR - BOTH VERBAL AND WRITTEN

Now ready to become associated with a progressive, growth-oriented
company where basic needs for challenge exist.

-1-

A few accomplishments........

RECOVERED $2,000,000 AT NORMAL OPERATING COST

As a patent attorney for my company, I was involved in major litigation brought in the Court of Claims against the U. S. Government. This constituted the infringement of a patent owned jointly by my firm and another company.

Prior to my participation in the suit, outside counsel had already billed legal fees in excess of $250,000. Counsel also estimated spending an additional $150,000 to properly conclude the litigation in the best interests of my company. They also felt that plaintiffs would be fortunate to recover ultimately the legal fees alone.

In my investigations, I worked closely with financial executives in the various divisions of my and other companies. In addition to other legal functions, it was necessary to search out and find particular invoices and review the general ledger books.

As a result of my direct participation in the discovery proceedings, we arrived at a settlement figure with the government. Instead of possibly breaking even as projected by outside counsel, we recovered in excess of two million dollars. The total cost to my company was merely the normal expense incurred by my department.

DESIGNED PRODUCTION AND TRUCK ENGINE BEARINGS

My assignment as a product engineer was to design and solve many sleeve bearing problems in connection with all types of power equipment.

It was necessary to participate in the computerization of many of the calculations which were involved in detailed engine load and lubrication analyses.

Due to my familiarity with the hardware and operation of all major and accessory power equipment, I designed for my company all automotive and truck engine bearings for a major car manufacturer for their model years 1974 - 1976 inclusive.

EARNED OVER $2,000 ANNUALLY IN
PRIVATE PART-TIME LAW PRACTICE

From 1973 to 1978, I handled all aspects of general legal work in private practice on a part time basis. I billed in excess of $2,000 annually. The majority of my practice involved wills, probate matters, estate planning, real estate transactions and personal injury work.

-2-

90

TREATISES WRITTEN ON FOREIGN LICENSEES
RESULT IN BETTER BUSINESS RELATIONSHIPS

One of my company's foreign licensees, located in Brazil, was threatening to terminate its contract because of poor understanding of the agreement and lack of communication regarding the venture. A newly appointed international vice president decided to employ someone with the necessary legal, manufacturing and business skills to compile a compendium which would update the licensee agreements not only of the Brazilian venture, but also of all the other foreign licensees. I was assigned to coordinate this extensive project to overcome licensee dissatisfactions.

In order to research information, it was necessary to maintain close contact with the top executives of both the licensees and my company. Treatises were prepared by me for all the foreign manufacturing joint ventures in South America, India, Japan and Italy. These "bibles" were approximately 80 pages in content. They recorded the complete chronology of events from the initial idea and contact, through the start-up, the attainment of regular production, and finally the showing of profits.

In addition to the chronology of events, these "bibles" included financial information, abstracts of the technical service agreements, licensing agreements, know-how agreements, trademark and trade-name user agreements, and all other agreements of legal significance.

As a direct result of the information I compiled in these treatises, our company was able to maintain better communication and relationship with all the foreign bearing licensees.

PROFESSIONAL AFFILIATIONS

American Bar Association
Baltimore Patent Law Association
Maryland Bar Association
Patent Office Society

PERSONAL DATA

Age 33   Married - one child   Willing to Relocate

References on Request

BUSINESS HISTORY

PATENT EXAMINER   1978 - Present

U.S. Patent Office
Washington, D.C.

PATENT ATTORNEY

TECHNICAL SYSTEMS ANALYST

PRODUCT ENGINEER   1972 - 1978

PRODUCTION & ENGINEERING TRAINEE

Champion Manufacturing Corporation
Baltimore, Maryland

MILITARY RECORD

U.S. Army   Technical Sergeant   1966 - 1967

EDUCATION

B.S. MECHANICAL ENGINEERING   1971

Massachusetts Institute of Technology

LLB (JURIS DOCTOR)   1973

George Washington University
National Law Center

NUMEROUS OTHER COURSES AND SEMINARS INCLUDING BUSINESS SUBJECTS

-4-

ROBERT A. BECK, Jr.
307 West Glenwood Avenue
Montgomery, Alabama 35217
205 - 871-2938

MANAGER - COMPUTER PROGRAMMING/STAFF ASSISTANT TO PRESIDENT

FOR FINANCIAL INSTITUTIONS

Experienced in Computers As:

Manager...Designer...Organizer...

...of Systems and Procedures

Fully Knowledgeable In:

Automating Departments...Evaluating Needs and Equipment...Systems and Procedures

Training and Orientation of Personnel...Conversion Operations

Served As:

Trust Officer..Operations Officer..Planning Officer..Executive Assistant

Well-Rounded Knowledge of Banking......Defining and Achieving Objectives

Proven Ability in Administering Trust Accounts

Managing People

INNOVATOR...............ADMINISTRATOR...............IMPLEMENTOR

-1-

A FEW ACCOMPLISHMENTS........

DESIGNS AUTOMATION OF TRUST DEPARTMENT!

When the bank decided to automate the Trust Department, I was assigned the responsibility of designing the System and effecting the conversion. Initially, it was a two-year project.

As my work progressed in the system design and records preparation, delivery time for the equipment was frequently moved up. With no extra employees, all personal trust accounts were converted to the machine system, and functioning effectively, within 13 months at a saving of considerable time and money. The department continued to grow at an annual rate of 10%, yet it operated with fewer employees. Due to my program of employee training and development of supervisors and administrative officers, I was able to take over additional administrative duties and personally handle a large number of Trust Accounts.

DEVISES CHECK SALES PROGRAM WHICH REDUCED STANDARD MATERIAL COSTS FROM $250,000 to $25,000!

While serving as Manager of the Computer Processing Department, I instituted and received management approval of a Check Sales program designed to obtain the necessary machine acceptability of all checks and deposit slips, and at the same time, reduce the expense of furnishing these items, which at the time would have cost $250,000.

The program proved extremely successful, as costs of supplying these items decreased to $25,000 per year as a result of the sales program.

CONDUCTS AUTOMATION CONFERENCE PROVIDING GUIDANCE TO CORRESPONDENT BANKS ON CONVERSION!

A major objective of the Computer Processing Department, under my management, was to provide guidance in the area of automated services to correspondent banks. Because of the lead time necessary for correspondent banks to get ready for conversion to automated systems, I successfully urged management to allow me to set up a conference to guide them in their development program.

Materials were prepared, an agenda established, speakers selected and a 100-page handbook was distributed to participants. Numerous visual aids, displays and equipment demonstrations by manufacturers augmented the presentations.

The conference was a complete success. Typical of the reaction of the more than seventy conferees was: ".....sincere congratulations on the manner in which your Automation Conference was conducted and for the thoroughness in which the subject was presented.....".

-2-

BUSINESS HISTORY

FIRST NATIONAL BANK OF MONTGOMERY   1967 - Present
Montgomery, Alabama

                  Manager of Data Processing - 2 years
                  Trust Officer - 5 years
                  Assistant Trust Officer - 3 years
                  Auditing Department - 2 years

SEARS ROEBUCK & COMPANY   1965 - 1967
Birmingham, Alabama

                  Department Manager

THE LANE AGENCY   1974 - 1965
Birmingham, Alabama

                  Salesman, Casualty Insurance and
                        Performance Bonds

UNIVERSITY OF ALABAMA   1962 - 1964
Tuscaloosa, Alabama

                  Research Assistant, Bureau of
                        Business Research

MILITARY RECORD

U.S. AIR FORCE   1955 - 1958

                    First Lieutenant (Pilot)
            Lt. Colonel, Air Force Reserve (Current)

EDUCATION

B.S. BUSINESS ADMINISTRATION   1959

M.B.A.   1962

                    University of Alabama

ADDITIONAL:

        IBM Management Courses
        General Electric 400 Programmer Course
        Command Staff School - U.S. Air Force

PERSONAL DATA

Age - 45   Married - 3 Children   Willing to Relocate
                                              and Some Travel

References on Request

CARL F. WAGNER
2510 ROSEMARY STREET
ROCHESTER, NEW YORK 14624
716 - 221-5907

PERSONNEL DIRECTOR

Broad Associations In

PERSONNEL MANAGEMENT & ADMINISTRATIVE SERVICES

ORGANIZATIONAL PLANNING & CHARTING

WAGE & SALARY ADMINISTRATION

MANAGEMENT DEVELOPMENT

PERSONNEL INVENTORIES

TRAINING PROGRAMS

BENEFIT PROGRAMS

JOB EVALUATION

-1-

.....Some "Personnel" Accomplishments

SALARY SURVEY INNOVATIONS DRASTICALLY REDUCE TECHNICAL AREA TURNOVER

Information on technical salaries from other major companies consisted of occasional mail surveys. Technical people were paid on this basis for lack of a better approach. The technical managers placed little confidence in this method.

As Manager of Salary Administration, I set up a classification system and recommended the granting of increases based on merit rather than the existing policy of length of service. I convinced management that visiting other firms to exchange salary and wage information was a practical solution to the haphazard system then in use.

As a result of these innovations, we won the support and confidence of the technical management group. The turn-over in the technical area has been extremely low ever since.

DEVELOPED PROCEDURES MANUAL ASSURING UNIFORM POLICY INTERPRETATION

The many facets involved in the area of centralized administration and the sizeable number of people administering the programs permitted several different interpretations of policies and procedures.

To offset this confusion, I produced a well documented and illustrated standards manual which thoroughly and completely outlined each and every one of the procedures.

This manual proved most helpful both in the training of new personnel in the department, and in assuring uniform interpretation of policy follow-up.

GOAL AND TARGET DATE PROGRAM INCREASES EFFICIENCY OF STAFF

Functionally, each of the nine division administrators under my supervision had definite assignments, but there were no goals set against which results could be measured.

A program was initiated wherein a goal as well as a target date was established for each administrator.

Results have been very gratifying in that more and better work was accomplished. The general attitudes and morale were also improved. Although the work load has been increased by one third since the inception of the program, the size of the staff has remained constant. As work volume increased, it was absorbed through a greater degree of over-all effectiveness.

BUSINESS HISTORY

MANAGER, PERSONNEL ADMINISTRATION   1974 - Present

                        The Whiting Corporation
                        Rochester, New York

MANAGER OF SALARY ADMINISTRATION   1965 - 1974

                        Computex, Incorporated
                        Lock Haven, Pennsylvania

CORPORATE PERSONNEL STAFF   1963 - 1965

                        Smith Manufacturing Co.
                        Philadelphia, Pennsylvania

EDUCATION

UNIVERSITY OF WASHINGTON   1959

            B.B.A. - Major Personnel Administration

                Various Other Courses In
        Law - Industrial Engineering - Finance - AMA Seminars

MILITARY RECORD

United States Army   Captain   1959 - 1963

MEMBERSHIPS

            Personnel Managers Association
            American Compensation Association

PERSONAL DATA

Age - 45   Married - 4 Children   Willing to Relocate

References on request

DAVID A. WALTERS
5206 N. 67th Street
Brookfield, Wisconsin 53219
414 - 355-1778

CASUALTY

CLAIMS MANAGER

Skilled In All Phases Of Claims Administration Including -

.. HANDLING AND SUPERVISION OF CLAIMS

.. CONTROL AND DIRECTION OF LITIGATIONS

.. RECRUITING/TRAINING OF ADJUSTERS

.. OFFICE PROCEDURES AND SYSTEMS

.. IBM 1400 RAMAC DATA PROCESSING

Well Educated (Speaks Five Languages) With Ph.D. Degree In Political Science And A Law Degree. Also A Chartered Property And Casualty Underwriter.

Equipped To Make Significant Decisions At High Management Levels.

Willing To Invest Skills And Talents With Progressive Growth-Minded Organization For Greater Management Career Opportunities.

. . . . .A FEW ACCOMPLISHMENTS

ESTABLISHES HIGHLY EFFICIENT NEW UNIT

Becoming a Resident Claims Manager, I was given the assignment to establish a
new claim unit involving the complete organization of work flow, the introduction of new methods, procedures, filing, systems and operations. Previously most of these activities were handled by phone and letter to distant
offices. Although I hired new personnel, several mediocre adjusters were
transferred to my division.

A Home Office audit, ten months later, showed my unit exceptionally well operated. The work load and pending files were reduced and efficiency increased.
My five adjusters received one "Excellent", three "Very Good", and one "Good"
rating. In the previous year, one of my men presently rated "Very Good" had
been placed on probation for poor performance, and the rest had been rated
"Average" to "Good".

REDUCES STATE MOTOR VEHICLE DEPARTMENT COMPLAINTS TO ALMOST ZERO

Constant friction existed between my company and the State Motor Vehicle Department. Company personnel corresponding with the Department failed to adhere to rules and regulations. A great deal of unnecessary correspondence
resulted in delays and ultimate loss of goodwill on the part of State officials. I was asked to analyze the situation and take whatever corrective
steps were necessary.

I held a series of personal conferences with the General Counsel and his staff.
Reviewing the applicable statutes, I drafted a comprehensive set of rules and
instructions to be used by the Company's personnel when dealing with the
Department. All Claims Supervisory Personnel were advised to comply with
these rules.

As a result of these activities, complaints emanating from the Motor Vehicle
Department have almost completely disappeared, with a corresponding drop in
unnecessary and time consuming letter writing.

SUCCESSFULLY TRAINS ADJUSTERS FOR ADVANCEMENT

During my seven years as a Claims Manager, I saw three of my adjusters promoted to Claims Managers in other States. No other Manager could match this
record in the Company.

Six adjusters whom I had recruited, trained and supervised in a former unit
over four years ago, are still members of the same unit under my successor.
During the same period, however, other units showed a turnover of from 25%
to 150%.

BUSINESS HISTORY

CLAIMS MANAGER   1973 - Present

Major National Insurance Co.
Milwaukee, Wisconsin

EDUCATION

PhD - POLITICAL SCIENCE   1968

University of Innsbruck
Austria

JURIS DOCTOR   1973

University of North Dakota

VARIOUS OTHER COURSES AT:

Marquette University Law School

Vale Technical Institute

LANGUAGES

FLUENT IN:

English - German - Hungarian

FAMILIAR WITH:

French - Italian

PROFESSIONAL MEMBERSHIPS

Society of Chartered Property Casualty Underwriters

Wisconsin Claims Council

Southern Wisconsin Claim Mens Association

PERSONAL DATA

Age - 37   Married - No Children   Willing to Relocate

References on Request

RICHARD E. SEMPLE
13432 FLORISSANT AVENUE
ST. LOUIS, MISSOURI 63116
314 - 355-7189

MARKETING RESEARCH EXECUTIVE

TECHNICAL-ECONOMIC ANALYST

Management Decisions Relying On My Evaluations
Covered A Wide Range of Subjects Including:

- . FLUID METERING

- . IN-LINE BLENDING

- . AUTOMATED DATA ACQUISITION SYSTEMS

- . FREQUENCY CONVERTERS

- . WASTE DISPOSAL

- . WATER TREATMENT

- . AGRICULTURAL STORAGE

- . THERMOELECTRIC DEVICES

- . REFRIGERATION

B.S. Degree In Chemical Engineering With Additional Courses In
Metallurgy And Cost & Statement Analysis Accounting.

Excellent Communicator - Verbal and Written.

Now Ready For Greater Career Potential With Progressive,
Growth-Oriented Company

. . . . . .A FEW ACCOMPLISHMENTS

MAKES MARKETING POTENTIAL STUDIES TO EVALUATE THERMOELECTRIC EFFECT

The Research Department was working on the development of semi-conductor materials for a popular energy conversion phenomenon, the thermoelectric effect. Thousands of dollars a year were spent on this project when I was assigned to evaluate some of the applications of thermoelectric effects.

My studies pointed out that considerable engineering development was required before the materials could be used in products; that the materials would be limited to specialty applications for many years because of economic considerations; that the company was not oriented to marketing low volume specialty items; and that if there was continued corporate interest in thermoelectric effects, effort should be concentrated on applicatons development rather than materials research.

This series of studies led to the termination of all research on thermoelectric effects. Events since have proved this to be a wise decision.

SAVES THOUSANDS OF DOLLARS ON NON-PROFIT PRODUCING RESEARCH

The fuel cell was being studied in one of the company's laboratories. The engineer was successful in developing electrodes for good performance, but only in half cells and under no-load conditions.

My assignment was to design a laboratory model fuel cell with high enough power output to allow significant tests under load conditions.

Under my direction, the laboratory model was built and a number of tests run. I prepared a comprehensive report which defined the engineering problems and gave detailed estimates of time costs and man power required to solve these problems. I pointed out that other companies had groups of over 100 engineers working to solve the engineering problems with limited success, whereas my company had at most only 2 engineers.

After evaluating this report, the company decided not to go ahead with the project, thereby not only saving thousands of dollars on this type of research, but also freeing research time for better assignments.

REDESIGNS WATER TREATMENT DEVICE MEETING ALL REQUIREMENTS

A water treatment device was brought to the attention of the company. The device was shown to be effective in the prevention of scale formation in evaporative coolers, bottle washing machines, etc. The inventor had been manufacturing this device on a low volume basis. However, the device was ineffective in that leakage currents existed between the electrodes and the case.

At this point I was assigned to design and build a unit which would eliminate the leakage. I redesigned the unit, retaining the basic principles involved, despite a tight time schedule.

As a result, all the requirements were met and the unit performed satisfactorily.

-2-

BUSINESS HISTORY

ANALYST-TECHNICAL ECONOMICS   1974 – Present

Danville Corporation
St. Louis, Missouri

INSPECTION ENGINEER   1969 – 1974

Universal Powder Company
Canton, Ohio

EDUCATION

B.S. CHEMICAL ENGINEERING   1969

University of Illinois

METALLURGY   1969 – 1973

Washington University
(Evening Division)

COST & STATEMENT ANALYSIS ACCOUNTING   1973 – 1976

Washington University
(Evening Division)

Various other courses and seminars

ASSOCIATION MEMBERSHIPS

National Association of Corrosion Engineers

American Institute of Chemical Engineers

PERSONAL DATA

Age – 36   Married – 3 Children   Willing to Relocate

References on Request

LEONARD M. JEFFERSON
7902 Mt. Prospect Road
Silver Spring, Ohio 30268
302 - 459-8720

CHIEF INDUSTRIAL ENGINEER

Broad, diversified background in Industrial Engineering
and Management activities of major operations,
both foreign and domestic.

Versatile and creative with an outstanding record of cost
reduction effectiveness in all areas of management.

EXPERIENCED IN:

....Industrial Engineering (Electro-Mechanical)
....Methods and Systems
....Products and Processes
....Computer Programming
....Management Organization
....Contract Administration
....Acquisition and Lease Negotiations
....Budgets and Costs
....Policies and Procedures
....Personnel and Manpower

FAMILIAR WITH:

....Marketing
....Sales Planning
....Product Lines
....Technical Processes

A PERSUASIVE COMMUNICATOR - - - BOTH VERBAL AND WRITTEN

A SYSTEMATIC PLANNER - - - ORGANIZER - - - IMPLEMENTOR

A FEW ACCOMPLISHMENTS

Saved hundreds of thousands of dollars below estimated budgets, not only in acquisition and leasing of sites, but also in manpower, material and equipment.

Resolved a highly critical production packing problem, while at the same time, saving almost $100,000 per year in labor costs.

Created and installed a new processing system and control mechanism which eliminated a heavy backlog and completely stopped excessive overtime.

Devised a series of changes to a labor accounting system which provided the costs of standby time and other kinds of delays.

Installed a punch-card system which processed during the night so that job performance information became available before the crews went to work in the morning.

Improved the appearances of facilities while achieving yearly savings of $40,000 on power and over $200,000 on maintenance and heat.

Developed labor standards separating labor by craft which resulted in better maintenance productivity.

Increased by 50% the number of line items per man in inventory control. At the same time eliminated overtime and overcame dissatisfaction of personnel.

Devised the basic specifications for computer system which controlled over 800,000 stock locations; pre-located material receipts; adjusted inventories; planned shipments; and made follow-ups to be certain that material was actually shipped.

Devised and implemented safety methods to substantially reduce accidents.

BUSINESS HISTORY

CHIEF OF INDUSTRIAL ENGINEERING   1973 – Present

AIR-STAFF INDUSTRIAL ENGINEER

U.S. Air Force
Washington, D.C.

CONSULTING ENGINEER   1965 – 1973

A.K. Moulton Associates
San Antonio, Texas

MANUFACTURING AND   1959 – 1965
APPLICATION ENGINEER

General Electric Co.
Schenectady, N.Y.

EDUCATION

BACHELOR of SCIENCE DEGREES in
ENGINEERING and ENGINEERING MANAGEMENT

(MIT) Massachusetts Institute of Technology   1959

MASTER of SCIENCE   University of Southern California   1973

Numerous special courses including computer programming, Information Systems
and Materials and Processes.

PROFESSIONAL AFFILIATIONS

American Institute of Industrial Engineers
American Management Association
American Institute of Plant Engineers
Far East Society of Architects & Engineers
Registered Professional Engineer

LANGUAGES

Speak understandable Spanish and Japanese

PERSONAL DATA

Age 45   –   –   Married – 5 children   Willing to
Relocate & Travel

References on request

JOHN E. LINTON
611 SOUTH EAST AVENUE
ROCHESTER, NEW YORK 14624
716 - 422-5457

F A C T O R Y   M A N A G E R

Broad Manufacturing Background In -

FINISHED AND SEMI-FINISHED METAL PRODUCTS

MECHANICAL POWER TRANSMISSION EQUIPMENT

MACHINE TOOLS - APPLIANCES

COST AND PROFIT-ORIENTED ABLE EXECUTIVE WITH PROVEN
CAPABILITIES IN TOP MANUFACTURING AND ADMINISTRATIVE
AREAS, INCLUDING MANAGEMENT/LABOR CONTRACT NEGOTIA-
TIONS.

NOW READY FOR GREATER CAREER OPPORTUNITY WITH PROGRES-
SIVE, GROWTH-MINDED ORGANIZATION WHERE ALL HIS SKILLS
AND TALENTS WILL BE FULLY UTILIZED.

A FEW ACHIEVEMENTS

OVERCOMES VOLUME LAG AND INCREASES PRODUCTION BY 60%

When I joined the company as Factory Manager, the shop was unable to produce sufficient volume to stay current with order requirements. This was primarily due to poor scheduling techniques, inadequate tooling preparation and supervision which was inept in planning and directing shop operations.

To overcome this condition, I instituted loading of work by machine centers and revised scheduling procedures. To obtain greater machine utilization, a second shift was added. Daily checks were made to assure that tooling and machinery were ready when needed. By reducing lost time, productive efficiency was increased.

With these changes, we were able to raise production by 60%, thereby producing the necessary volume of work to meet order requirements.

REDUCES EXPENSES TO STAY BELOW BUDGET

Manufacturing expenses were more than 140% of the budgeted standard. It became my responsibility to hold expenses within the budgeted level.

After instituting weekly status reports on key supply items in order to follow trends, I analyzed monthly variances by account and took immediate corrective steps to bring excessive ones back in line.

As a result of the above and other actions, the ratio of direct to indirect personnel was improved, thus earning greater burden absorption. The manufacturing department expenses were reduced to 90% of budget in my first year of operation responsibility.

NEGOTIATES SUCCESSFUL MANAGEMENT/UNION CONTRACT THROUGH IMPROVED RELATIONS

The company had just experienced a six week strike and labor relations were still strained when I became associated with the organization. As management labor negotiator, I was determined that both company and union would adhere to their contractual obligations, and that management rights would be asserted.

Keeping in close touch with all concerned, I saw to it that problems were handled promptly. The company's position and its basis in the contract and precedent were clearly defined.

Gradual improvement became evident in management/union relations. These relations were put to the test when contract negotiations were again begun. The company wanted a two-year contract with maximum 2½% package annual increase. I successfully negotiated a settlement, and a new agreement was signed on the company's terms. A noteworthy result of the good relations established was that my shop employees had the highest per capita contribution of all manufacturing companies in the city during the latest United Fund Drive.

-2-

BUSINESS HISTORY

FACTORY MANAGER   1975 - 1982

Rochester Bearing Corporation
Rochester, New York

MATERIAL CONTROL MANAGER   1971 - 1975

Underwood Manufacturing Co.
Kankakee, Illinois

PRODUCT ENGINEER   1966 - 1971

Sanders Manufacturing Co.
Frankfort, Indiana

PROCESS ENGINEER   1965 - 1966

Ingram Manufacturing Co.
Evansville, Indiana

MANUFACTURING FOREMAN   1964 - 1965

Andrews Refrigeration Co.
Evansville, Indiana

EDUCATION

B.S. CERAMIC ENGINEERING   1962

University of Illinois

MASTERS DEGREE - BUSINESS ADMINISTRATION   1964

Harvard University

PERSONAL DATA

Age - 43   Married - 3 Children   Willing to Relocate

References on request

RAYMOND E. RONALD
710 SOUTH EVANS ROAD
SKOKIE, ILLINOIS 60634
312 - 557-3210

P L A N T   M A N A G E R

with well-rounded experience...

in operations

  Production

  Maintenance--Equipment and Facilities

  Methods and Standards

  Personnel

  Union Negotiations

  Cost Control

  Purchasing

  Quality Control

  Production and Inventory Control

in engineering

  B.S. Degree--Mechanical Engineering

  Product Design Engineering

  Production Design Engineering

  Process Engineering

  Plant Layout Engineering

  Sales Engineering

creative planner...efficiency-oriented...effective leader...

A FEW ACHIEVEMENTS

REDESIGNED PRODUCT AND PRODUCTION METHODS- - - -

INCREASES PRODUCTION BY 150%

Additional production was needed to supply the demand for one of the company's lines.

I felt that this could best be accomplished by a redesign of the product, so it would lend itself to more modern manufacturing processes.

I redesigned the product, keeping all of its quality features. I also re-aligned production procedures, redesigning and adapting existing equipment and consolidated operations.

Actual unit production on this line of products was increased by 150% without any plant expansion or major capital expenditures.

STREAMLINED PRODUCTION - - - -

SAVES $130,000 in LABOR COSTS

It was my feeling that production costs could be reduced by proper labor and machine utilization.

I, therefore, undertook a complete survey of operations by departments, re-evaluated personnel and established a minimum operational level for each category. I devised a comprehensive production scheduling system, tying it into a material control system.

This streamlining of production methods and controls reduced labor costs alone by $130,000 in the first year.

ENGINEERED NEW PRODUCT - - - -

CREATES NEW GROWING MARKET

It became apparent to me that the company could produce new products within their existing facilities.

After surveying the market and state and local municipality requirements, I engineered a product utilizing existing manufactured components. Prototype samples were approved for market testing and governmental approval. The results of these steps indicated a substantial potential.

With a tooling expenditure of only $12,000, the company has sold over $400,000 worth of these products in the past two years, and future sales volume seems assured.

-2-

BUSINESS HISTORY

GENERAL PLANT MANAGER   1976 - Present

James Corporation
Chicago, Illinois

CHIEF ENGINEER   1970 - 1976

Skokie Engineering Company
Skokie, Illinois

ENGINEER   1970 - 1976

Universal Refrigeration Systems, Inc.
Chicago, Illinois

EDUCATION

B.S. MECHANICAL ENGINEERING   1966

Illinois Institute of Technology

MASTER - BUSINESS ADMINISTRATION   1968

Northwestern University

ASSOCIATIONS

American Institute of Mechanical Engineers

Registered Professional Engineer

PERSONAL DATA

Age - 38   Married, 2 Children   Willing to Relocate

References on Request

CHARLES C. ARNOLD
315 Forest Avenue
Springfield, Massachusetts   01105
413 - 626-2011

CHIEF TOOLING OR MANUFACTURING ENGINEER

METAL WORKING AND DIE INDUSTRIES

WITH EXCELLENT POTENTIAL TO PLANT MANAGER

SOLID BACKGROUND

... TECHNIQUES

   ... DEEP DRAWING

      ... BULGING

         ... ROLL FORMING

            ... TRIMMING AND BEADING

               ... INSIDE FINISHING

                  ... BUFFING

                     ... HELIARC AND STUDWELDING

                        ... STAMPING

                           ... ASSEMBLY

EQUIPMENT -

... TOGGLE AND HYDRAULIC PRESSES

   ... STRAIGHTSIDE AND O. B. I. PRESSES

      ... ACCESSORIES (FEEDS, STRAIGHTENERS, ETC.)

      ... COIL HANDLING EQUIPMENT

         ... SEMI-AUTOMATIC AND AUTOMATIC BUFFERS

SKILLED IN ORIGINAL DESIGN, DEVELOPMENT AND PRODUCTION

AN ORGANIZER   -   A LEADER   -   AN ADMINISTRATOR

-1-

114

A FEW ACCOMPLISHMENTS

OVERCOMES BULGING PROBLEMS ON STAINLESS STEEL PRODUCTION

The addition of stainless steel items manufactured by my company brought a whole new area of problems in bulging. Under the increased pressure needed to bulge stainless steel, the rubber heated up very rapidly and tended to break down after only a few pieces were formed. Various methods and types of rubber used only created more problems.

Experimenting with urethane, which was used in brake forming, I felt that if it worked in a press brake, it should also work in bulging. After many tests by increasing the clearances and using different lubricants, results became highly satisfactory.

My company is now using urethane as the exclusive medium for bulging on both stainless steel and aluminum. Although double the cost of rubber initially, it out-lives rubber by a minimum of a 10 to 1 ratio. In addition, complex shapes which were not considered feasible previously, are now in production.

ELIMINATES AN ANNEALING PROCESS IN PRODUCTION OF STAINLESS STEEL PERCOLATORS

With the increased popularity of stainless steel, my company decided to produce a stainless steel percolator in addition to their line of aluminum ones. They found, however, that two intermediate anneals were required to produce the percolator in accordance with the desired design and the use of conventional drawing methods.

No facilities existed in the plant for annealing. It was necessary, therefore, to pack and send out the shells to a commercial source. These extra operations forced a rise in the production costs to where the product became overpriced against competition.

By departing from the conventional methods and through the use of reverse (inside-out) drawing procedure, I was able to eliminate one anneal.

The resultant savings made the stainless steel percolator more competitive and it is now one of the company's major products. From what was learned on the percolator, it became simple to add a stainless steel urn to the line.

REDUCES SCRAP LOSS FROM 29% TO LESS THAN 1%

My company started to use a new 3-ply metal (stainless steel as the two outer layers and aluminum in the center for good heat transfer) for the cookware line. This metal does not have the good drawing qualities normally associated with stainless steel. In forming the sharp hollow required, scrap was running at 29%. Management finally realized the futility of such an operation, and I was assigned the task to correct this costly condition.

After studying the situation, I increased the shoulder diameter of the pan and eliminated the hollow. This formed a flat in the shoulder so that a proper fitting cover could still create a satisfactory water seal for waterless cooking.

Before changing the complete line, I ran a test production on one item. This turned out a scrap loss of less than 1%. Currently, production on all items in the line have been changed with similar scrap loss results.

- -

BUSINESS HISTORY

CHIEF TOOLING AND MANUFACTURING ENGINEER   1965 - Present

Royal Ware, Incorporated
Springfield, Massachusetts

EDUCATION

BS MECHANICAL ENGINEERING   1965

Columbia University

Various Other Technical and Administrative Courses

ASSOCIATIONS

American Society of Tool & Manufacturing Engineers

MILITARY RECORD

U.S. ARMY AIR FORCE   First Lieutenant (Navigator)   1959 - 1965

PERSONAL DATA

Age - 41   Married, 5 Children   Willing to relocate

References on request

ROBERT S. SCHMIDT
102 Snydor Drive
Milwaukee, Wisconsin 53231
414 - 920-1052

MANAGER

STRUCTURAL STEEL FABRICATION

WITH DOMESTIC AND FOREIGN EXPERIENCE

Broad management background and technical knowledge in all phases of construction, fabrication and refabrication of structural and reinforcing steel.

RESPONSIBILITIES INCLUDED:

...Plant Layout and Erection
...Purchasing
...Warehousing facilities
...Inventories
...Sales
...Personnel
...Contract Negotiations

COST-CONSCIOUS AND PROFIT-ORIENTED

SYSTEMATIC PLANNER - ORGANIZER - IMPLEMENTOR

A MULTI-LINGUIST

A few accomplishments...

-1-

BUILT STEEL PLANT SHOWING PROFIT
AFTER YEAR OF OPERATION

My company decided to establish a subsidiary division to produce both reinforcing and structural steel. As General Manager, my assignment was to
start from scratch, locating a site for the operation, and layout and build
the plant.

I made a search for a suitable location and found an ideal site containing
13 acres. The plant was built to my specifications. I designed the con-
veyor systems and ordered all the necessary machinery.

The first year of operation, the plant produced 4700 tons of reinforcing
steel and 1500 tons of structural steel. The second year, reinforcing steel
production rose to 11,000 tons. Although earnings were not projected for
the second year, the operation did make a healthy profit. Incidentally, I
personally contacted customers and sold the entire output of steel produced.

REORGANIZED STRUCTURAL STEEL DEPARTMENT
FROM LOSS TO PROFIT OPERATION

A fabricating steel company was losing money when I was installed as General Superintendent. The production set up was deplorable and jammed in
all directions. A large contract was 60 days behind schedule and back
charges from the erector amounted to almost 10% of the total contract price.
Due to faulty fabrication, shipments were delayed and some were incomplete.

After studying the situation, it was necessary to reorganize the entire
structural department. I redirected the flow of material and gave overhead
cranes specific areas of operation. The inventory and warehousing were re-
arranged. Fabrication was closely inspected. Visiting the erector, I corrected on-the-spot problems with him.

As a result of the improvements, the production line operated properly within a period of two months. The major contract was completed only 30 days
behind schedule with back charges reduced to a minimum. Steel was fabricated according to specifications. Revised loading and shipping procedures
expedited shipments. Capacity was increased, thereby decreasing the cost
per man per ton fabricated.

-2-

OVERCAME LOCAL DIFFICULTIES AND
CONSTRUCTED RAILROAD ON SCHEDULE IN BRAZIL

When I was placed in charge of steel construction of a railroad in Brazil, I found the workmanship was very poor. The steel was not fabricated according to plans and specifications. Most of the steel for the bridges, hoppers, switch controls and signal towers was fabricated in Brazil.

To correct the condition, I set up a complete on-job-site refabrication plant to rework the steel received. This helped to remedy the inconsistencies of the local production. My knowledge of the language proved invaluable in working with the Brazilian people. The railroad was completed on time and I was rewarded with a considerable bonus for my efforts.

- -

BUSINESS HISTORY

VICE PRESIDENT & GENERAL MANAGER	1979 - Present
White Construction Company Milwaukee, Wisconsin	
GENERAL MANAGER	1972 - 1979
Brookville Steel Corporation Brookville, Ohio	
GENERAL SUPERINTENDENT	1967 - 1972
Steel Fabricator Corporation Hanover, Pennsylvania	
CONSTRUCTION SUPERINTENDENT	1961 - 1967
Franki LeDeux Antwerp, Belgium	

EDUCATION

TOYAL ATHENEUM - Hasselt, Belgium	1962
MODERN BUSINESS SCHOOL - Brussels, Belgium	1963
ECOLE COLONIAL - Leopoldsville	1964
Various Business and Technical Courses in United States	

PROFESSIONAL AFFILIATIONS

American Institute Steel Construction
Concrete Reinforcing Steel Institute
Association Steel Fabricators
American Welding Society

PERSONAL DATA

Age - 43   Married - 3 Children   Willing to Relocate
Domestic or Foreign

References on request

-3-

DENNIS H. REESE
2129 SPRING STREET
FORT WORTH, TEXAS   76114
817 - 272-3946

Q U A L I T Y   C O N T R O L   E X E C U T I V E

-Who knows the importance of this
function in controlling costs
and satisfying customers

EXPERIENCED IN . . .

. Quality Control Supervision

. Production Supervision

. Engineering Supervision

. Design Engineering

. Product Designing

. Research Design Engineering

. Service Engineering

. Technical Writing

. Service Instruction and Training

THE BACKGROUND NECESSARY TO EFFECTIVELY CONTROL QUALITY . . .

QUALITY ASSURANCE PROGRAM REDUCES COSTS - SECURES 92% RELIABILITY RATING

As Quality Assurance Engineer, I was given the responsibility of supervising this function at a facility producing an important Polaris component.

I found that suppliers were using different processes. By standardizing these procedures, cutting down machine time, suggesting improvements in handling and storage, changing final inspection to the night shift so as to allow the use of test fixtures during the day to check progression, we were able to make substantial cost savings. In addition, reliability and quality were greatly improved.

The result --- our company was able to reduce its price by 50% on these parts, we were given a 92% Reliability rating, and we maintained a quality rating of .42 discrepancies per unit.

BREAKS DOWN ENGINE IGNITION SYSTEM - FINDS CAUSE AND CORRECTION OF SALES HINDERING DEFECT.

When a new line of internal combustion engines came off the line, we found that they had a high speed miss.

Endeavoring to locate the cause, I disassembled the ignition system and checked all moving parts against the drawings. They all checked out and functioned according to specification. I innovated a series of test devices and found that the miss was not constant but varied from cylinder to cylinder. Further investigations pinpointed the problem to the breaker points.

From the information I supplied, the trouble was traced to the springs on the breaker points where it was found that the supplier had made a miscalculation.

New springs, properly made, were secured and the problem was eliminated.

ESTABLISHES QUALITY CONTROL AND RELIABILITY SECTION - CREATES SUBSTANTIAL COST SAVINGS.

Our company secured a contract to produce an important component for the B-58 aircraft. I was given the responsibility of creating the quality control and reliability programs necessary to achieve the successful completion of this contract.

Starting with our suppliers, we surveyed their facilities, briefed them on the required standards and established quality control procedures, forms and methods.

A reliability study was undertaken and the various systems involved were analyzed. In this fashion we were able to determine ahead of time where malfunctions could occur. New hardware and/or methods were devised to remove this possibility.

82% of all potential discrepancies were eliminated before production started. And--the company was able to reduce estimated costs by several million dollars.

BUSINESS HISTORY

QUALITY ASSURANCE SUPERVISOR   1969 - Present

Crowell Manufacturing Company
Dallas, Texas

DESIGN & RELIABILITY SUPERVISOR   1962 - 1969

Otis Aviation Corporation
Denver, Colorado

QUALITY ASSURANCE MANAGER   1959 - 1962

American Aircraft Corporation
Dallas, Texas

RELIABILITY SUPERVISOR   1957 - 1959

Longbon Manufacturing Company
Fort Worth, Texas

EDUCATION

BS - ELECTRICAL ENGINEERING   1957

Carnegie Mellon University

PROFESSIONAL

Joint Engineers' Council Manpower Commission
American Institute of Aeronautics and Astronautics
Society of American Military Engineers
Technical Writer including published papers on Gravities
Public Speaker appearing before Civic and Technical Groups
Holder of 48 U.S. Patents

PERSONAL DATA

Age - 50   Married, 2 Children   Willing to Relocate

References on Request

HENRY D. CARPENTER
5666 North Glenwood Avenue
Toledo, Ohio 43615
419 - 788-0618

PRODUCTION SUPERVISOR

QUALITY CONTROL ENGINEER

Broad Experience And Educational Background

In

METAL FABRICATION

AND

ASSEMBLY

With Knowledge Of

TAPE CONTROLLED MACHINES AND AUTOMATIC COMPUTERS

* COST ORIENTED

* SAFETY CONSCIOUS

* PLANNER AND IMPLEMENTOR

* SKILLED WRITER

A FEW ACCOMPLISHMENTS . . . .

NEW INNOVATION INCREASES PRODUCTION AND SAVES $33,000 ANNUAL LABOR COSTS

As Punch Press Department Supervisor, I noticed that each operator went to the die crib when he finished his job to return his tools. Then the operator would proceed to the planning crib to obtain his next assignment. This practice resulted in much productive time lost due to personal and interference delays.

I devised a system wherein the new job assignment and tools were personally delivered to the operator prior to the completion of his current job. A messenger would also pick up along the way, tools for return to the die crib.

This innovation was evaluated by an industrial engineer who made actual time measurements and computed savings for the operation. His study showed a saving of $33,000 labor cost the first year! In effect, production time was increased by this amount.

REDUCES OPERATING PROBLEMS TO ROUTINE MAINTENANCE

The Chief Process Engineer was not satisfied with the amount of time taken to produce a new product after initial design. I was given the assignment to submit a program to correct this situation.

Upon investigation, I discovered that long delays resulted from the confusion caused by blaming the operating department for new tool failures. I recommended shifting the responsibility of producing good tool parts back to the departments which built them, thereby making them aware immediately of their own mistakes. In addition, this program called for both dimensional and operational acceptance of each new tool before submittal to the production department.

With this program in effect, weeks of lost time disappeared in the production of new products, and operating problems in the production area were reduced to routine maintenance. Customer promised delivery dates were thereby maintained on schedule!

ELIMINATES AMPUTATION ACCIDENTS THROUGH USE OF NEW DEVICE

In the Punch Press Department, the major cause of finger amputations was due to machine failure. The operator's hand would get caught in the die as the machine repeated its cycle. This was a very expensive accident for both the operator and the Company. Fatigue cracks in the tripping, rolling key clutch usually turned out to be the source of the failure.

I recommended the use of an ultra-sonic crack detection device to check machines without incurring expensive teardowns. This device could also be used on new clutches received from the manufacturer to detect any defects. After a successful trial period, the Vice-President of Manufacturing agreed to the purchase of this detection device.

As a result of the installation, the average of 3 amputations per year caused by machine failure has been entirely eliminated with obvious beneficial effects to both the operators and the company.

BUSINESS HISTORY

PRODUCTION SUPERVISOR

1977 - Present

Morrison Manufacturing Co.
Toledo, Ohio

INSPECTION SUPERVISOR

1975 - 1977

General Stove Corporation
Evansville, Indiana

EDUCATION

B.S. MECHANICAL ENGINEERING

1971

University of Minnesota

Various Additional Courses including Automatic Computers

MILITARY RECORD

U.S. AIR FORCE

1971 - 1975

2nd Lieutenant

AFFILIATIONS

American Society of Tool and Manufacturing Engineers

American Society of Quality Control Engineers

PERSONAL DATA

Age - 34   Married - 4 Children   Willing to Relocate
and Some Travel

References on Request

WILLIAM C. BEYER
9164 ARTHUR STREET
SOUTH BEND, INDIANA 46615
219 - 272-3625

D I R E C T O R

RESEARCH AND DEVELOPMENT

In The Field Of

PLASTIC ENGINEERING

Highly Qualified In:

TECHNIQUES

PROCESSES

METHODS

EQUIPMENT

Associated with Plastic Engineering

Ph.D. - CHEMICAL ENGINEERING

One Of The Few Scientists With Practical Working Knowledge

And Experience In The Extrusion Of Vinyl Dry Blends And

In The Use Of Dielectric Heat Sealing

Solved Variety of Technical Problems...Helped To Make Many

Marginal Processes Successful In The Introduction And

Promotion Of New Products

AN INVENTOR   AN ORGANIZER   AN ADMINISTRATOR

A FEW ACCOMPLISHMENTS . . . . .

INSTALLS NEW PROCESS WHICH SAVES OVER $300,000 ANNUALLY

For many years, my company purchased all the vinyl film and sheeting used to fabricate inflatable toys, wading and portable swimming pools. I suggested an investigation into the merits of producing the film and sheeting instead of purchasing them and was given the assignment to evaluate the economics of doing this on a profitable basis.

My evaluation indicated an expected return of between $100,000 and $150,000 during the first year of operation. Based on this evaluation, the company installed an extruder along with other equipment and facilities for dry blending vinyl compounds. I worked up the plans, ordered the equipment, drew up the plant layout, made up and tested suitable formulations. In addition, I directed the installation of the equipment and the training of crews to operate it.

One year after the first pound of film was extruded, we produced about 2,000,000 lbs. at a saving of approximately $200,000 and a better quality film. Also about 350,000 lbs. of scrap was recovered and extruded into film worth $120,000. This utilization of scrap film resulted in a net saving of approximately $100,000.

ESTABLISHES PRODUCT DEVELOPMENT DEPT. RESULTING IN MANY "FIRSTS."

The company decided to establish a product development department for long-range planning in the plastics division. The purpose was to create and develop new products, and develop prototypes and processes for the production of these new products. I was assigned the responsibility to establish this department.

I organized the department, hired engineers, artists and supporting personnel. This group created up to 150 new items and designs for an inflatable toy line and wading and swimming pool lines.

SOME "FIRSTS" AS A RESULT -----

** The first in the industry to produce a swimming pool selling for less than $100.00.

** The first to construct pools from vinyl-coated welded wire mesh and vinyl impregnated nylon or dacron.

** The first to design, produce and market an inflatable "punching bag" toy.

** The first to compound a vinyl film, for use in making liners for pools lasting more than 5 years, when exposed to sunlight in southern areas such as California, Florida and Arizona.

MANY OTHER ACHIEVEMENTS INCLUDE SEVERAL PATENTS!

BUSINESS HISTORY

LINTON PLASTICS INDUSTRIES, INC.   1957 – Present
South Bend, Indiana

Director of Research & Development	1977 – Present
Director of Development	1975 – 1977
Manager Special Projects & Processes	1969 – 1975
Plant Manager	1966 – 1969
Production Manager	1959 – 1966
Electrical & Special Projects Engineer	1957 – 1959

EDUCATION

B.S. CHEMISTRY   1953

University of Pennsylvania

MASTERS – FOOD & SANITARY BACTERIOLOGY   1955

University of Michigan

PhD – CHEMICAL ENGINEERING & SANITATION   1957

University of Michigan

Various other courses in Management

PROFESSIONAL ASSOCIATIONS

American Chemical Society

Society of Plastic Engineers

PERSONAL DATA

Age – 52   Married – 3 Children   Willing to Relocate
and Travel

References on Request

JOHN F. CHRISTENSON
11765 Tulane Avenue
Long Island, New York 11107
212 - 416-2695

MANAGER OF INDUSTRIAL ENGINEERING

Broad, diversified background in industrial engineering and management activities of major multi-divisional companies.

Versatile and creative with an outstanding record of cost reduction effectiveness in all areas of management.

KNOWLEDGE OF:

...Technical Processes
...Methods
...Research and Development Activities
...Management Organization

EXPERIENCED IN:

...Industrial Engineering
...Financial Management
...Contract Administration
...Budgets and Costs
...Policies and Procedures
...Personnel

FAMILIAR WITH:

...Marketing
...Sales Planning
...Product Lines
...Development

A SYSTEMATIC PLANNER -- ORGANIZER -- IMPLEMENTOR

A PERSUASIVE COMMUNICATOR -- BOTH VERBAL AND WRITTEN

A few accomplishments....

-1-

IMPROVED METHODS REDUCE LEAD TIME 28%
AND LABOR REQUIREMENTS 20%

A large metal fabricating concern was encountering fierce price and delivery competition. Production was behind schedule and a major customer threatened to cancel all future business unless deliveries were accelerated. My assignment was to find a way to significantly reduce time in order to be competitive.

A study was made in detail of the que, flow and operation time from the starting activity to the shipping date of the accepted product. Another study involved the over-all plant layout, scheduling process, material and work flow, equipment utilization and identification of key suppliers. My recommendations were accepted for both the improvements in methods and the required educational process involved at the group level.

Over a six month period, lead time was reduced 28% and labor requirements 20%. The resultant accelerated deliveries remedied the major customer complaint. As a by-product, a larger percentage of the industry volume was obtained because of the greater cost-effective capacity realized.

RECOMMENDATIONS FOR A VARIABLE OVERHEAD
BUDGET SYSTEM NOW USED BY ENTIRE CORPORATE ORGANIZATION

Rising overhead costs in a large metal and fiberglass division of a multi-divisional corporation were threatening the company's competitive position. Their share of the market was slipping and cost levels were preventing them from realizing a profit on current work.

As an on-site management consultant, I studied the company's overhead costs, pools, trends and allocation models. I carefully analyzed current and projected sales forecasts, work load and skill requirements. My recommendations were accepted for a variable overhead budget system based on objective labor requirements by skill category. A training course was designed and introduced for use and understanding of overhead-type work measurement and variable budgeting.

As a direct result, management was able to reduce overhead personnel levels by 40%, reduce overtime and provide better service through improved job definition, methods, systems and procedures. This approach has since been incorporated as the way to do business for the entire corporate organization.

NEGOTIATED COST REDUCTIONS AMOUNT TO 40% PER UNIT

My assignment was to independently evaluate a contractor's cost performance on a complex manufactured electronic product, and estimate an objective price as opposed to an historical one, for the production version of this product. Based on these findings we were to provide technical support in presenting these findings and achieving the predicted results.

The study included an evaluation of how the contractor planned, budgeted and controlled his work. The product and its manufacturing process were reviewed, including all of the "shop paper" used in fabricating, assembling and testing. My findings and recommendations were then presented to our client for negotiation with the contractor. I also participated in the negotiations.

The negotiated cost reductions ran into the millions of dollars on the basis of an approximate 40% reduction in unit cost. In addition, guaranteed performance warrantees were obtained and an improved management control system installed.

Some More Accomplishments

Designed a computerized cost and proposal analysis (CPA) system which provided extremely rapid and effective cost and trade-off analyses for improved management decision making. This approach is now included in a military film identifying better cost and management control.

Reduced the labor cost 35% for a large diversified manufacturing company by balancing the workforce to the workload through improved methods and scheduling and in the reduction of overtime hours from 8% to 2%.

Recommended and helped put into effect a 50% unit cost reduction on a combustible equipment item through improved labor and material standards and more effective use of plant and equipment to reduce overhead costs.

Introduced a new concept called "Earned Value" which is used as a yardstick to periodically measure performance and program status on a routine basis as related to actual cost versus achievement. Specific problems were identified much earlier in the development cycle affording management quicker ability to take corrective and preventive actions. The Department of Defense has adopted the "Earned Value" concept as a contractual requirement with all major firms.

Made a study for a large rubber company producing fabricated parts who found their competitive cost position in jeopardy. Instituted a program calling for variable budgets based on labor standards, improved shop loading and scheduling techniques, problem identifications and follow-up systems. Result was a 65% reduction in direct labor hours per unit and a 25% reduction in overhead cost. Improved quality and a 10% reduction in leadtime were additional fringe benefits.

-3-

BUSINESS HISTORY

CHIEF INDUSTRIAL ENGINEER   1972 - Present

Industrial Consulting Company
New York, New York

MANAGEMENT ANALYST   1970 - 1972

Staley Manufacturing Company
Springfield, Ohio

MANAGER PROFIT CONTROL   1967 - 1970

Chamberlin Products Corporation
St. Louis, Missouri

EDUCATION

B.S. INDUSTRIAL MANAGEMENT   1964

Carnegie Mellon University

MASTERS DEGREE - BUSINESS ADMINISTRATION   1967

University of Maryland

NUMEROUS OTHER COURSES AND SEMINARS

PROFESSIONAL AFFILIATIONS
American Institute of Industrial Engineers (AIIE)
Society for Advancement of Management (SAM)
American Association for Advancement of Science (AAAS)

PUBLICATIONS
Several articles in the Journal of Industrial Engineering
and other business publications

PERSONAL DATA

Age - 41   Married - 2 Children   Willing to Relocate
                                                    and Travel

References on Request

-4-

JESSE L. RONALD
1645 Crestline Road
Sunnyvale, California 94087
805 - 684-1615

ENGINEERING MANAGEMENT

In the Fields of

Chemical Engineering - Processing - Product Development

DIVERSIFIED EXPERIENCE IN:

....Direction and Coordination of Major Projects
....Chemical Research and Development
....Ordnance
....Solid Propellants

DETAILED KNOWLEDGE OF:

....Organic and Inorganic Oxidizers
....Synthetic Rubbers
....Exotic Metals
....High Energy Fuels

INVOLVED IN:

A PROFIT-ORIENTED CHEMICAL ENGINEER WHO HAS DIRECTED ACTIVITIES

OF ELECTRICAL, CHEMICAL AND MECHANICAL ENGINEERS IN MAJOR

PROJECTS, ALONG WITH MANAGEMENT OF PLANT PERSONNEL.

AN ORGANIZER   A PROBLEM-SOLVER   AN IMPLEMENTOR

-1-

A FEW ACCOMPLISHMENTS . . . . .

ESTABLISHED COMPETITIVE BIDDING SYSTEM SAVING OVER $500,000 ON ONE PRODUCT ALONE

During development work for a large Air Force contract, my company had consistently purchased ammonium perchlorate from one source, upward of 500,000 pounds at $28\frac{1}{2}$ cents per pound.

As part of my work on this project, I realized our needs could run in excess of five million pounds of ammonium perchlorate and strongly urged evaluation of other sources for this and other materials, with the result that competitive bidding was established for vendors.

The low bidder, with an acceptable product, was awarded the contract at $18\frac{1}{2}$ cents per pound, realizing a saving in excess of $500,000 on this one chemical. Additional savings were experienced in other chemicals such as aluminum powder, epoxy resins and polybutadiene fuels. Total savings resulting from this investigation exceeded one million dollars.

RESOLVED TECHNICAL PROBLEMS TO EXPEDITE PRODUCTION ON URGENTLY NEEDED HIGH ENERGY SYSTEM!

There was an urgent need for a large solid propellant rocket. However, only an antiquated development facility was available. The time schedule was extremely short for reactivating the facility, designing and installing new equipment, and successfully extruding the unit. An all-out effort was required by the resources of an entire Propulsion Development Department.

Named Coordinator of the Project, I selected a task team of Electrical, Mechanical and Chemical Engineers, Designers and Draftsmen, along with other technical personnel to carry out the task. I selected leaders to carry out various sub-tasks, reviewed the progress and redirected the efforts as necessary on a daily basis, working very closely with all plant personnel involved.

Although faced with many seemingly unresolvable technical problems at the beginning, the project was successfully accomplished ahead of schedule, with all assigned goals completed.

CORRECTED HAZARDOUS PROBLEMS IN EXTRUSION PROCESS FOR SOLID PROPELLANTS!

The Army and Navy had been working for many years on the development of a continuous extrusion process to replace the batch ram extrusion process. The results were negative, with many fires and explosions interfering with the research and development phases of the work.

While working at the Naval Ordnance Test Station, I was assigned as manager of the project. I discovered that the basic problem and cause of fires was due to rubbing contact between the screw and barrel of the extruder. This caused no problem when working with plastic, but the extrusion of a friction-sensitive material, such as propellant, was extremely hazardous. After redesigning the screw and die, and installing certain safety devices, extrusion was accomplished.

The extruder was built and performed successfully. The result was a superior product, with only one-third the rejects of the old method, and a 25% saving in cost. I received a Superior Accomplishment Award from the Navy for the success of this project.

-2-

134

BUSINESS HISTORY

MANAGER OF ENGINEERING   1976 - Present
and MANUFACTURING

United Technology Center
Sunnyvale, California

ENGINEERING MANAGER -
PROCESS DEVELOPMENT

Rocketdyne, Inc.   1973 - 1976
McGregor, Texas

MANAGER OF DEVELOPMENT   1970 - 1973
ENGINEERING

Northrup Carolina, Inc.
Asheville, North Carolina

PROGRAM MANAGER   1965 - 1970

Naval Ordnance Test Station
China Lake, California

EDUCATION

B.E. CHEMICAL ENGINEERING   1965 -

University of Illinois
School of Engineering

A.A. ENGINEERING   1961 -

Wright Junior College

Various other courses including Management and Supervisory.

PUBLICATIONS

Various publications including "Industrial and Engineering Chemistry".

AFFILIATIONS

American Chemical Society - Senior Member
American Institute of Aeronautics and Astronautics
American Ordnance Association

PERSONAL DATA

Age - 40   Married - 4 Children   Willing to Relocate
                                                     and Travel

References on Request

ALFRED A. SIMMONS
2114 Marion Avenue N.W.
Indianapolis, Indiana 46263
219-233-4551

ENGINEERING EXECUTIVE

Experienced -

. . . . GENERAL MANAGER

. . . . OPERATIONS MANAGER

. . . . SALES ENGINEER

Young, 36-year-old dynamic self-starter with exceptionally

broad experience in many areas of management.

B.S. degree in Mechanical Engineering. Economy-oriented.

Steady, solid history with one company.

Now ready to become associated with a progressive,
growth-minded organization where my many skills
will be utilized to the fullest advantage for long-
range career opportunities.

. . . . SOME REPRESENTATIVE ACCOMPLISHMENTS

REHABILITATION PROGRAM PRODUCES MORE SALES AND BETTER COMPANY IMAGE

Assuming duties as Operations Manager, I found some 400 outlets in my division nearly 100% inadequately equipped and poorly maintained. This presented a poor company image, with a resultant deterrent to sales.

I reviewed specific requirements for each location with field engineers to obtain the most efficient equipment and improvements within a designated budget. Long-range planning upgraded the locations on the most deserving-first basis and continued over a three-year period with new methods utilized to effect savings.

Currently, these outlets are among the best in sales volume in the company and very competitive in appearance. Equipment is on a scheduled replacement cycle, with maintenance costs per outlet reduced through planned preventative measures.

AUTOMATIC SYSTEM PROPOSAL REDUCES OVERHEAD AND FREIGHT RATES

Distribution terminal loading required the use of personnel on a 24-hour basis to obtain maximum potential of the facilities. This was too costly with infrequent pickups, so some terminals were available only during scheduled hours. Company, customer and carrier trucks could not make full use of their equipment, resulting in expensive idle time.

I proposed automatic systems for controlled access and loading at terminals on a 24-hour basis without the assistance of company personnel. Upon proposal acceptance, I installed specialized equipment using coded cards for identification and computing quantities received.

This resulted in reduced overhead, a 10% lower freight rate and better customer service. On a long-range program, a feed into central IBM will cause quicker billing of accounts with resultant savings in interest. In addition, sales personnel can better evaluate the sales market through earlier availability of reports.

MATERIAL HANDLING INNOVATION SAVES FLOOR SPACE AND INCREASES STORAGE AREA

While my company had palletized many warehouse items, there was no effective setup for tires, batteries and accessories due to the difficulty in stacking this type of merchandise.

After surveying all available material handling equipment and techniques, I developed a stackable pallet designed to hold ten tires vertically. The pallet parts were designed to be mass produced and shipped knocked down, with easy assembly in the warehouse.

The first completely palletized accessory warehouse in the company was thus established. A 50% saving of floor space was gained, while available storage space was increased about 250%. Over-all warehouse operation became more efficient, requiring fewer men to operate.

-2-

BUSINESS HISTORY

ACME CHEMICAL COMPANY   1972 – Present
Major Chemical Processor and Distributor
Indianapolis, Indiana

      DIVISION OPERATIONS MANAGER – 5 Years

      TERMINAL MANAGER – 3 Years

      FIELD CONSTRUCTION ENGINEER – 1 Year

MILITARY SERVICE

U.S. AIR FORCE   1965 – 1968

      Master Sergeant

EDUCATION

B.S. MECHANICAL ENGINEERING   1972

      University of Kansas

PROFESSIONAL MEMBERSHIPS

      Indiana Petroleum Council

PERSONAL DATA

Age – 36   Married – 1 Child   Willing to Relocate

References on Request

SAMUEL C. WILLIAMSON
7901 EDGERTON AVENUE
ALLENTOWN, PENNSYLVANIA 18104
717 - 421-5359

GENERAL PLANT MANAGEMENT

C H I E F   E N G I N E E R

MECHANICAL   - - - - -   INDUSTRIAL

YOUNG, DYNAMIC EXECUTIVE WITH BROADLY DIVERSIFIED

MANAGERIAL EXPERIENCE IN A MULTI-DIVISION ELECTRI-

CAL AND MECHANICAL DEVICES MANUFACTURING COMPANY.

VERSATILE AND CREATIVE WITH AN OUTSTANDING RECORD

OF EFFECTIVENESS AS A PROBLEM-SOLVER IN ALL AREAS

OF PLANT MANAGEMENT AND LABOR RELATIONS.

NOW READY TO STEP INTO A POSITION OF BROADER RESPON-

SIBILITY FOR A PROGRESSIVE COMPANY WHERE PROVEN

SKILLS AND ABILITIES CAN BE OF VALUE IN OVER-ALL

CORPORATE GROWTH.

-1-

139

A FEW ACHIEVEMENTS . . . . .

DEVELOPED STANDARD DATA PROGRAM WHICH SAVED $725,000

When I became Chief Process Engineer, there were no adequate cost controls for the manufacturing operations. Cost figures were available, but because of lack of control, they were not reliable. Labor costs were therefore well above the budget level.

Making an analysis of the existing Standard Data Program, I determined that the system had been designed for only 45% coverage of direct labor. Many of the standards were unrealistic and the system was completely confusing. I also learned that management was not sold on the existing program and that the program had been started and stopped several times. Parts of the data in use had been set by various consultants from different firms thus causing inconsistencies in the standards.

It was necessary to reorganize the entire department. I introduced MTM and trained the Standards Engineers in its use as a check system (not for setting standards). Under my supervision, the old standards were updated, new data was set and a new Standard Data Program was developed, implemented and expanded to over 85% coverage.

Thereafter, annual savings on Total Manufacturing Direct Labor were estimated to be: 1965 - $300,000; 1966 - $300,000; 1967 - $125,000. This outstanding accomplishment earned me another promotion.

RECOMMENDS USEFUL INDIRECT LABOR COST CONTROLS - SAVING $225,000 YEARLY

As Chief Process Engineer, it was my responsibility to evaluate control of indirect labor. I found that efficiencies were low as measured by my check studies. I also noted that supervisors lacked knowledge that would enable them to improve this performance.

After evaluating a number of existing programs, I recommended installation of two separate programs for the main areas. For unskilled operations such as material handling (including stockroom and truckers), the WOFAC program was selected. For tool making and other skilled more precise functions, the A.T. Kearney measurement program was decided upon.

As a result of the installation of these two systems, combined savings reached $225,000 annually.

INSTITUTES TRAINING PROGRAM WHICH REDUCES EXPENSE RATES

When I was assigned as Manager of the Special Products Division, I found an organization lacking system and control because responsibilities had neither been understood nor delegated.

I devised, instituted and conducted a training program for supervisors outlining their responsibilities and the part they played in the total operation.

As a result of this program, there existed a better team effort with acceptance of responsibilties and a higher degree of morale in the Division. This
led to a reduced expense rate while still meeting production requirements.
Annual savings of $50,000 were estimated.

BUSINESS HISTORY

MANUFACTURING MANAGER   1976 – Present

Walters Manufacturing Company
Electrical–Mechanical Products
Special Products Division
Allentown, Pennsylvania

EDUCATION

B.S. MECHANICAL ENGINEERING   1972

Carnegie Mellon University

M.S. INDUSTRIAL ADMINISTRATION   1976

Ohio University

PERSONAL DATA

Age – 32   Married – 1 Child   Willing to Relocate

References on Request

CHARLES G. PURVIS
2291 Wildwood Avenue
Kankakee, Illinois 60925
815 - 932-2938

C H I E F   E N G I N E E R

With Depth in - -

Education and Experience

SOLID EXPERIENCE IN:

- Engineering Management
    - Research and Development
        - Production Engineering
- Design Engineering
    - Cost Control Engineering
        - Application Engineering
- Sales Engineering
    - Quality Standards Engineering
        - Project Engineering
- Product Engineering
    - Manufacturing Practices
        - Technical Writing

ACTION-ORIENTED . . . . RESULT-ORIENTED . . . . GROWTH-ORIENTED

-1-

A FEW ACCOMPLISHMENTS . . . .

KNOWLEDGE OF MODERN TECHNOLOGY SECURES $1,500,000 CONTRACT

As Chief Engineer, I made it a personal policy to keep my department abreast of new technological developments even though it did not appear at the time that there might be a use for them in the company. One such development was Plastic Encapsulating.

A large OEM account gave my company the opportunity to bid on their requirements. Included were a quantity of encapsulated motors which had to be delivered within six weeks.

Because I had kept the department so well informed, the company was able to meet the required delivery date and, as a result, secured this $1,500,000 contract.

REDESIGNED LIMITED PROFIT LINE WHICH SAVED $200,000 IN COSTS

Due to competitive conditions, the profit yield of a standard line of products dropped to 1%. I embarked on a program to reduce costs without affecting quality.

Analyzing all the component parts of the products, I soon pinpointed the areas that were overdesigned for the needs. Starting on a redesigning program, I was able to reduce the usage of material while maintaining quality and saleability.

Within six months, the newly-designed and thoroughly-tested products were in production. At the end of the year a savings of $200,000 had been accomplished.

REALIGNED MANPOWER - SAVED COSTS AND SECURED INCREASED DEVELOPMENT MAN-HOURS

When I, as Chief Mechanical Engineer, was assigned the responsibility of an engineering division, I found it operating over budget and behind on projects.

After delving into the problem, I selected all the routine positions of the work and established procedures that could be followed by technicians.

By having the technicians concentrate in these areas, the qualified engineers were released for the more complicated development work.

Within six months the division was operating on budget; there had been a savings of $12,000 in costs; and there had been a gain of 3,600 man-hours in development work.

BUSINESS HISTORY

CHIEF ADMINISTRATIVE ENGINEER   1974 - Present

The Morrison Manufacturing Co.
Kankakee, Illinois

VICE-PRESIDENT ENGINEERING   1967 - 1974

Benton Electric Motors Co.
Benton, Michigan

PROCESS DEVELOPMENT ENGINEER   1966 - 1967

Standard Motors Corporation
Chatanooga, Tennessee

EDUCATION

B.S. MECHANICAL ENGINEERING)
)   Ohio State University   1965 - 1966
B.S. ELECTRICAL ENGINEERING)

PROFESSIONAL ASSOCIATIONS

Registered Professional Engineer
Institute of Electrical and Mechanical Engineers
American Society of Mechanical Engineers

PERSONAL DATA

Age - 39   Married - 5 Children   Willing to Relocate

References on Request

-3-

144

MORRIS R. GILBERT
4527 Southland Avenue
Alexandria, Virginia 22320
703 - 354-9887

MECHANICAL ENGINEERING MANAGEMENT

MAINTENANCE & CONSTRUCTION

PROJECT - PLANT

Young, successful Engineer with nineteen years experience in the area of Industrial, Mechanical, Maintenance, Structural, Construction Engineering and General Plant Management.

Work association history with some of the foremost manufacturers in the food processing, building materials, chemicals and automotive industries.

Now ready to become a member of a progressive management team for a Company with growth potential. Willing to invest my talents and skills for long-range career opportunities.

-1-

A FEW ACHIEVEMENTS . . . . .

PLANNED MAINTENANCE PROGRAM SAVES PRODUCTION DOLLARS

My multi-plant employer did not have a planned maintenance program. It became my task to develop one and sell it to the various plant managements.

I instituted a program of work sampling, preventive maintenance, mechanical inventory control and corrective maintenance.

In two years time I increased the "Do Work" category in work sampling from 35% to 55% in plants employing over 100 maintenance personnel. The last evaluation showed annual savings of $850,000 for an expenditure of less than $20,000.

PLANNING LEADS TO DESIRED RESULTS

The company contracted to provide nylon tire cord to the tire industry from a plant that did not exist. Delivery was scheduled two years hence.

After preliminary planning and plant start-up, this left 18 months to construct a $125 million addition to an operating plant. As Project Manager, I planned and scheduled this work so that the addition was completed on time and within budgetary limits.

This accomplishment had been considered as an almost impossibility by some experts.

CAREFUL SELECTION OF ENGINEERS AND CONTRACTORS PAID OFF HIGHLY

Processing plant construction costs were running an average of X dollars per square foot prior to my association with the company.

In spite of an 8% rise in the construction cost index, the last four plants built were constructed for X minus 4% dollars or a calculated decrease of 12%. The main reason for this reduction was, besides better preliminary planning, the engineers and contractors which I carefully selected. "Extra" work was reduced to less than 1%.

FEASIBILITY STUDIES PREDICT RETURN ON INVESTMENT

During a two-year period, I made five studies of new projects.

Management decisions were made on the basis of these studies.

After a year and a half of operation, the costs were within plus or minus $1\frac{1}{2}$% of these studies.

-2-

BUSINESS HISTORY

MANAGER - MAINTENANCE & CONSTRUCTION   1973 - Present

                    Norman Corporation
                    Falls Church, Virginia

PROJECT MANAGER   1966 - 1973

                    B.F. Sandhauser Corporation
                    Decatur, Georgia

INDUSTRIAL ENGINEER   1963 - 1966

                    Chevrolet Motor Division
                    Janesville, Wisconsin

MILITARY SERVICE

U.S. NAVY   1959 - 1963

                    Lieutenant

EDUCATION

B.S. Mechanical Engineering   1959

                    U.S. Naval Academy

Other courses in Engineering and Business Administration taken at:

                    Massachusetts Institute of Technology
                    University of Wisconsin

PROFESSIONAL MEMBERSHIPS

American Society of Mechanical Engineers

PERSONAL DATA

Age - 45   Married - 2 Children   Willing to Relocate

References on Request

HERBERT E. BECK, Jr.
214 MARION STREET
ROCKVILLE, MARYLAND 20822
301 - 252-1465

SENIOR PROJECT MANAGER

SUCCESSFUL ENGINEERING AND ADMINISTRATIVE RECORD

CRYOGENICS AND CONSULTING

Preparation and Administration of Project Budgets

Maintenance of Construction

Manufacturing and Purchase Schedule

Administration of Contracts for

Equipment, Construction and Services

Knowledgeable

Construction	Cost Estimating	Schedules
Design	Industrial Engineering	Budgets

A MOTIVATOR   - - - - - -   AN ORGANIZER   - - - - - -   AN IMPLEMENTOR

148

A FEW ACCOMPLISHMENTS. . . . .

As senior project manager:

Initiated and supervised the design, construction and start-up of new air-separation plants. Consulted on a regular basis to manufacturing personnel for efficient and effective operations.

Organized new engineering department to advise manufacturing. Supervised cost estimates and proposals.

Supervised all phases of cryogenic engineering, planning schedules and budgets, and liaison between engineering, client, company officers, subcontractors, attorneys, unions and production.

Responsible for individual projects with costs of $4 million and supervision of 75 people.

As mechanical project engineer:

Supervised subcontracts on preliminary cryogenic work for NASA's Mississippi Test Facility. Responsible for operations of 20 engineers.

Organized and planned $25,000,000 brewery expansion including ammonia refrigeration, CO_2 liquefaction, beer and grain process flow with direct supervision of 200 engineers, draftsmen and construction personnel.

Prepared report for high altitude rocket test facility using large quantities of cryogenic fluids. Project cost $50,000,000 and responsible for 20 engineers and draftsmen.

Responsible for complete mechanical design for hyperballistic missile facility using high pressure hydrogen and helium compressor systems and large capacity low vacuum systems. Supervised 30 engineers and draftsmen.

Supervised 50 engineers and draftsmen on first high altitude rocket test facility designed for high pressure cryogenics and gases.

-2-

BUSINESS HISTORY

SENIOR PROJECT MANAGER   1977 - Present

Phelps Cryogenic, Inc.
Bowie, Maryland

MECHANICAL PROJECT ENGINEER   1964 - 1977
(Consultant)

Gunderson Engineering Company
Washington, D.C.

DRAFTSMAN   1962 - 1964

Danfield Consulting Company
Phoenix, Arizona

EDUCATION

B.S. MECHANICAL ENGINEERING   1962

Arizona School of Mines & Metallurgy

MILITARY RECORD

U.S. NAVY   Lieutenant   1954 - 1958

AFFILIATIONS

American Society of Mechanical Engineers

National Society of Professional Engineers

PERSONAL DATA

Age - 48   Married - 4 Children   Willing to Relocate

References on Request

-3-

PHILLIP A. HODOSH
5511 CAHILL ROAD
MINNEAPOLIS, MINNESOTA 55424
612 - 941-2329

E N G I N E E R

STRUCTURAL DESIGN, CONSTRUCTION AND R & D TESTING

Strong Background And Experience In:

PROJECT MANAGEMENT

STRESS ANALYSIS

HEAVY CONSTRUCTION DESIGN

RESEARCH & DEVELOPMENT

CONSULTING

ESTIMATING

SCHEDULING

TESTING

CONTRACTS

Cost-Conscious, Profit-Oriented And Extremely Knowledgeable
In All Phases Of Structural Design And Construction, Including
The Management And Sales Areas.

Now Seeking A Career Opportunity With A Growth Organization Where
My Many Skills And Talents Will Be Utilized To The Fullest Extent
To Complement The Management Team.

-1-

A FEW ACCOMPLISHMENTS

----- Have a patent pending for a new type of building block which eliminates the use of mortar and cuts construction time.

----- Contributed substantially to the development of data contained in the Concrete Reinforcing Steel Institute (CRSI) Design Handbook.

----- Saved one-half million dollars for the owner on a $5,000,000 multi-story hospital job by suggesting the changing from a steel frame to a concrete frame.

----- Developed engineering design constants derived from laboratory tests of Titanium that now have become company standards for Biaxial Gain Factors, Temperature Degradation Factors, Modulus of Elasticity in Biaxial Stress Fields and Poisson's Ratio.

----- Predicted where a beam would fail in a missile transfer handling system, but was overruled in the design. After it failed, I was given the assignment to correct the design.

By making the beam less rigid, I overcame the dynamic response caused by the rapid deceleration of the strongback which caused the beam to fall in torsion.

As a result, my company landed a $17,000,000 contract with the Navy.

----- Currently managing an $11,500,000 industrial process facility and responsible for the contracts involved. I not only wrote the many contracts because of my legal and technical background, but also assigned them to both prime and sub-contractors.

----- The list of successful achievements can go on and on!

-2-

BUSINESS HISTORY

PROJECT MANAGER   1977 - Present

Thor Manufacturing Company
Process Equipment and Systems Division
Minneapolis, Minnesota

R & D ENGINEER   1974 - 1977

Design and Test of Missiles
Aerosponic Corporation
Maywood, California

R & D ENGINEER   1972 - 1974

Dynamic & Stress Analysis of Machinery
General Dynamics
El Segundo, California

PROJECT ENGINEER   1967 - 1972

William R. Storan Associates
Consulting Engineers
Los Angeles, California

PROJECT ENGINEER   1965 - 1967

Heavy Construction Design
American Steel Corporation
Englewood, California

EDUCATION

B.S. CIVIL ENGINEERING   1965

Columbia University

LAW COURSES   Loyola University

ASSOCIATION MEMBERSHIPS

American Concrete Institute

Registered Professional Engineer in:
Arizona - California - Minnesota

PERSONAL DATA

Age - 39   Married - 5 Children   Willing to Relocate
                                                 including Abroad

References on Request

-3-

153

THE MOTIVATION LETTER

The "motivation letter" will be simple to write since the essentials can be copied from your resume. It should include several interest-creating points in order to arouse sufficient curiosity in your capabilities to excite the company. The letter should also show that you can make a profit or that you are a problem solver.

Your "career image" or immediate objective should be mentioned in the beginning. If education is of great importance in your field, then this information should follow next. Otherwise, education can be incorporated toward the end of the letter. Accomplishments (success stories) should be included in the body of the letter. Give reason for being unemployed. If employed, state "for valid reasons, I am seeking a change of position."

The letter should be one page in length whenever possible. Depending, however, on the position sought, you could describe your accomplishments to the extent of a page and a half. Your sentences should be short and to the point for easier readability and understanding.

Turn your negative drawbacks into positive statements, or rather omit any mention of them. For example, if you lack a college degree, either bypass mention of educational background or say something to this effect: "Self-educated, I rose from the bottom to my present position of treasurer." Do not mention age if you are over fifty years old, or else state that you are a "mature executive." If you are a young 45, say so.

You will note in the following examples of motivation letters that in no instance are they "begging" type letters. You are creating a desire for your product on its merits and its advantages to the potential buyer. Your request for an interview doesn't end with a "May I hear from you" plea. Neither do the letters contain self-appraisals such as "sincere, loyal, hard-working, honest, etc." These types of personal traits are taken for granted.

For small or medium size companies, the letters should be addressed directly to the President. In the very large or giant companies, it is best to address the letter to the Vice-President in charge of your particular field. If you are seeking an extremely high echelon position, then your letter should be sent directly to the President or Chairman of the Board.

Whether you are in Sales, Marketing, Finance, Manufacturing, Engineering, Administration or any other facet of business or industry, the ingredients recommended here should be incorporated in your motivation letter. Again, you will find it simple to write the letter since you already have the success stories and other information available from your resume.

Following are examples of successful motivation letters.

(Example 1)   LEONARD M. JEFFERSON
                               7902 Mt. Prospect Road
                             Silver Spring, Ohio   30268
                                  302 459-8720

                                                            Date

Mr. _____   (Title)
Company
Address

Dear Mr. _____:

Your organization may be in need of a top-level Chief Industrial Engineer who
has a highly successful background in major cost reductions and management
activities in the planning and implementation of domestic and overseas expansion facilities.

Due to conditions beyond my control I am seeking a position with an organization which will utilize my knowledge and experience to obtain a better competitive company position.

Young, age 45, I earned SB degrees in Engineering and Engineering Management
at M.I.T. I also have an MS in Aero-space Management from U.S.C. In addition, I have taken numerous special courses including Computer Programming,
Information Systems and Materials and Processes.

I have lectured on preventative maintenance of equipment and facilities at an
international conference for factory management executives. I speak understandable Spanish and Japanese.

You may be interested in some of my accomplishments:

            Created and installed a new processing system and control
            mechanism which not only eliminated a heavy backlog, but
            also completely stopped excessive overtime.

            Devised the basic specifications for a computer system which
            controlled over 800,000 stock locations; pre-located mater-
            ial receipts; adjusted inventories; planned shipments; and
            made follow-ups to be certain that materials were actually
            shipped.

            Saved hundreds of thousands of dollars below estimated bud-
            gets, not only in acquisition and leasing of sites, but also
            in manpower, material and equipment.

My wide range of experience enables me to ferret out technical and administrative problems and to muster the right resources to resolve them. I am
considered to be thorough in analysis and quick to grasp details.

If you desire to discuss my background and experience in greater detail, I
shall be pleased to do so in a personal interview.

                                    Sincerely,

(Example 2)
JOHN J. JONES
2345 Jarvis Boulevard
Port Smith, Ohio 22205
(123) 456 - 7890

March 12, 198__

Mr. R.L. Benson, Vice Pres.
Acme National Mfg. Co.
13422 Central Ave.
Cleveland, Ohio

Dear Mr. Benson:

As Senior Project Engineer in the electro-mechanical field, I have invented several products which are now in production. The patents pending are under my name for the companies involved.

I am writing to you because your company may be in need of an individual with my experience and training in the areas of Logic Design, Electronic Packaging, Instrumentation, Computers, Communications and allied fields. For valid reasons I am seeking a change of position. (Note: If unemployed, say, "Due to conditions beyond my control, I am currently unemployed.")

You may be interested in some of the things I have done:

--Under my direction and participation, we designed an electronic desk calculator with internal and external features not found in competitive machines. The machine is in production with an estimated yearly sales volume of around $20,000,000.

--I supervised the designs of installation hardware for a communication system costing one million dollars at each of three sites. A major accomplishment was that no rework was necessary on this job.

My degree in Mechanical Engineering was earned at Stevens Institute of Technology. I also have an M.S. degree in Applied Mathematics from Ohio State University. Various other courses have been taken to further my education.

If you desire to discuss my background and experience in greater detail, I shall be pleased to do so in a personal interview.

Sincerely,

(Example 3)

LEWIS MANTER
c/o Mother
ROSE MANTER
6821 E. Speedway
Tucson, Arizona 85712
602 - 364-8281

Date

Mr._____, President (or V.P.)
Name of company
Address

Dear Mr. _____:

Your organization may be in need of a young, age 36, top-level executive staff assistant who has a highly successful and diversified background in administrative and technical phases of corporate operations.

Currently, I am Senior Computer Control Supervisor for a firm in Zaire, Africa. For family reasons, I wish to return to the United States and become associated with a progressive organization where my many skills and abilities will be fully realized and utilized for career growth.

Prior to my present company, I was employed for 9 years with a firm in Okinawa. I was involved in various managerial and operational positions relating to all phases of data processing; systems analysis; logistics; technical services; material maintenance; property administration; liaison and other facets connected with an engineering organization. In addition, I was responsible for hiring personnel and creating on-the-job training courses.

In the course of my many assignments, I have interpreted and implemented programs towards developing profit while also serving to coordinate better long-range planning with scheduling of facilities, equipment and skills available and required.

I would like to discuss with you a more detailed account of my experience. You may reach me by writing:

Constructeurs Inga-Shaba
B.P. 15698
Kinshasa, Republique du Zaire, Africa

or contact me

c/o My mother's address and phone listed
on the letterhead.

Sincerely,

Resume attached

(Note - This is one of the very few times a resume is included with the
       Motivation Letter.)

(Example 4)

JANET HOLDEN
3219 S. Emerson Avenue
Dallas, Texas – 1265
(817) – 679-1265

Date

Mr. (Name) (Title)
Company
Address

Dear Mr._____:

My experience and expertise in the field of TV newscasting may be exactly what you are looking for.

Starting as a film processor after earning a BBA degree, I rose through various TV functions to become the news director for a medium-size Texas station.

Three years later, I was offered and accepted a position as newscaster for a major market area station in Texas. Subsequently, I received the Associated Press award for the best newscast in all of Texas. Incidentally, this NBC affiliate station also received the ARB rating as the highest rated newscast in the market area.

For valid reasons, I am now free to become the anchorwoman for a TV station where my many television skills and abilities will be fully utilized for future growth.

I would like to discuss with you how I can be of value to your station.

Sincerely,

(Example 5)

JOSEPH P. JOHNSON
4760 East Palmas Drive
Tucson, Arizona 85710
602 - 298-3405

Date

Mr. (name) (title)
Company
Address

Dear Mr. _____:

Your organization may be in need of a young man with my background and experience in the general fields of business and industry.

I have recently made Tucson my home and am seeking a position where my many skills and abilities may be utilized to the fullest extent for career growth.

Young, age 25, I have a B.A. degree in Political Science, but my business experience includes purchasing, production planning, accounting, office procedures and expediting. I am also acquainted with some phases of shop work.

I work well with management and am considered creative, a good planner, organizer and implementor.

I would like the opportunity to discuss with you a more detailed account of my background and how I can be of value to your organization.

Sincerely,

(Example 6)

JOHN J. JONES
2345 Jarvis Boulevard
Port Smith, Ohio 22205
(123) 456 - 7890

March 12, 198__

Mr. R.L. Benson, President
Acme National Steel Co.
13422 Central Ave.
Cleveland, Ohio

Dear Mr. Benson:

Your organization may be in need of a Structural Steel Fabrication Manager who has a highly successful background both in domestic and foreign operations.

I have just resigned as Vice President and General Manager of a family-owned contracting firm involved in the erection of steel structures. Prior to this position, I have been General Manager of both structural and reinforcing steel fabrication plants.

In the course of my foreign and domestic assignments, my positions included all phases of construction and steel fabrication for almost every type of end product from bridges to signal towers for railroads.

You may be interested in a few of my accomplishments:

--A young steel fabricating company was losing money with contracts behind schedule. In one instance, back charges from the erector amounted to 10 percent of the total contract. Taking charge as General Superintendent, I reorganized the entire production department, eliminating the jams by re-directing the flow of materials. At the end of 2 months, schedules became current and quality improved. Production was increased with resultant large savings on labor and material.

--Saved my company considerable money on foreign trips to purchase steel because of my multi-language fluency and knowledge of how to deal with foreign firms.

Young, age 44, I am Belgian born and educated. In addition, I have furthered my education with numerous technical and business courses in the United States.

I would like the opportunity to discuss with you a more detailed account of my experience.

Sincerely,

PRINTING OF PROMOTIONAL MATERIAL

A good 20 pound white rag bond paper should be used for the "motivation letter," and No. 10 envelopes. *Personal stationery is very necessary.* To save money, have a printshop print 200 sheets with just your letterhead when ordering the motivation letter. A fast letter-shop will do your work less expensively than a regular printer. Also order 200 extra envelopes, so that you will have business-like stationery for your personal correspondence with companies.

The 4-page foldover resume should be printed on heavier 60 pound stock and in a light color, not necessarily white. The 2-, 3-, or 4-single page resume, however, should be on white stock using the same 60 pound paper.

An IBM (or other good make) typewriter should be used for both the motivation letter and the resume. A good typist is all you need. When the letter is printed, leave space to fill in the individual's and the company's name and address and the "Dear Mr._____" salutation. The typist will date the letter, fill in what is needed and address the envelopes from the 3 × 5 cards you prepared. This person can also fold, insert, seal, stamp and mail the letters.

Personally sign each letter. A good typist combined with a good letter-shop will make each letter become an individual personal one, which is what you want the recipient to believe.

THE MAILING LIST

Refer back to the Summary pages starting on page 23 in the section on "Career Goals." You have by now determined the type of industry, size of company and geographic location which fit your needs. This knowledge is necessary in the make-up of your mailing list.

Every industry, no matter what its function, is classified under an SIC code number. SIC stands for "Standard Industrial Classification." These codes are prepared under the sponsorship and supervision of the Office of Statistical Standards of the Bureau of the Budget, Executive Office of the President. The SIC codes cover every type of enterprise, whether it is mining, agriculture, manufacturing, wholesale, retail, services, etc. All reference books such as *Dun & Bradstreet, Standard & Poor, Moody's,* etc. list these code numbers. Your library usually has these reference books, along with a copy of the *Standard Industrial Classification Manual* issued by the Bureau of the Budget.

It is simple, therefore, to create a mailing list based on SIC numbers for your particular purpose. Dun & Bradstreet's *Million Dollar* and *Middle Market* directories are recommended for making up the list. Other mailing sources can be found in directories published by trade journals or trade associations in your field of endeavor. Also, there are *Directories of Manufacturers* by state available at your Chamber of Commerce or public library.

Another source for top-level management position seekers is Dun's *Reference Book of Corporate Managements* which lists the top 1,000 companies with the names and brief histories of their senior executives. Most reference directories are available at your main library. Banks and brokerage firms will have some of these directories. You may have to write for specific trade or trade association directories.

(*Note:* We do not advise the purchasing of names from a list house. No such list purchased will be as complete or up-to-date for your individual need as the one which you prepare yourself.)

You will experience no difficulty in finding your SIC classifications. For example, the industrial code number for chemicals is SIC 28-12 through 28-99. If this is your industry, you can select the types of products with which you are familiar from within this category.

In your search for SIC categories, do not limit yourself to just one. Take into consideration alternative functions in which you have experience or knowledge. Refer to the "Desirability and Availability" section, page 21. You will probably find additional SIC categories which match your other types of background. Your present field may be in rubber manufacturing, but there are other areas such as plastics where your experience would apply.

In your selection of companies, do not be too discriminatory. Check them on the basis of volume, number of employees and geographic location per your self-appraisal. Do not try to evaluate 100 or more companies on what you may have heard about them. Obtain the interview, and then determine for yourself the make-up of the company. Your opportunities may be affected by being too choosy in developing the mailing list.

Mergers have resulted in the formation of divisions within corporate structures. As a rule, divisions are practically autonomous in operation and should be considered as individual companies of medium size. Therefore, you may write to individuals in several divisions within a major corporation if your technical or administrative background lends itself to them.

On a separate 3 x 5 card, print just the name of the company when scanning through the SIC sections of the directories. At this point this is all the information you need. When you are through with all the company names on the cards, alphabetize them. Then turn to the alphabetical section of the directory for further information concerning the size, volume and geographic location. As you select the company for the mailing list, complete the 3 x 5 card by adding the company address and the name and title of the president or senior executive to whom you will address the letter. Print (do not write) so that the typist will have no difficulty in reading the card. No one likes to see his name misspelled.

The 3 x 5 card makes it easier for the typist to address the letter and the envelope. A card should read like this:

```
Mr. R. L. Benson, President
Acme National Mfg. Co.
13422 Central Ave.
Cleveland, Ohio   22205
```

ANSWERING ADS

The Personnel Manager becomes involved only after management decides the need for a position to be filled. He does not create the opening. It is his responsibility to obtain a pool of candidates from which the right man will be selected.

His first step is to review the qualifications with the executive to whom the prospective employee will report. In addition, he may have job specifications to refer to. Once he knows all about the position and type of person required, a "Position Available" ad will be composed and inserted in the paper, usually under a blind box number.

If you are employed, there is a very slight risk of replying to your own company's ad but the odds are greatly in your favor that it is not your own company. If you personally answer a blind ad, there is no way to maintain anonymity. A third party approach may be used wherein a friend replies to the ad for you by saying he knows someone who fits the requirements. You will thus maintain anonymity and possibly find out the name of the company. Responses are generally very poor when this method is used, and therefore it is not recommended.

Replies to ads may sometimes run well over 1,000 depending on the type of position available, the media used for coverage, and the size of the ad. Obviously only the personnel department can handle such a quantity and therefore they do the initial screening. The first step necessitates a favorable acceptance by people who composed the ad and know what the specifics are. Experience has proven that responses to an ad received immediately upon publication get a quick scanning to determine whether the specific requirements have been complied with. Obviously with large quantities of replies to read, the personnel department quickly sorts out those letters which do not pass their own test factors.

The best time to reply to an ad is between one to two weeks *after* publication. Your letter will then receive closer attention. Even if other applicants have had interviews, a final decision is seldom reached before weeks and perhaps months have elapsed. Do not be afraid that you have been eliminated because of a late reply. The higher the position, the longer it takes to arrive at a decision.

Whereas your motivation letter was sent to a narrow select group of companies in your specific "career image" field, you should broaden your scope in answering ads. If the ad touches any part of your experiential background, reply to it even if you are not in the age or salary range specified. Age is relative and can be overcome in an interview, and salary is negotiable.

Your letter should try to answer *every specific* mentioned in the ad with the exception of "salary requirement" and the request for a resume. *Under no circumstance do you send a resume.* You want the interview and your reply should create the interest for it. Revise your motivation letter to fit the ad requirements and make it brief. Your letter has to single you out among the hundreds of replies which are received.

Do not start your letter with "In reply to your ad, etc." It is obvious this is why you are sending it. Refer to the examples of motivation letters starting on page 155. In replying to an ad by Example 1, the writer should begin with the second paragraph stating "Due to conditions beyond my control, etc." The letter should then follow with specific accomplishments which apply to the requests in the ad.

In Example 2, the letter should start with the first paragraph, "As Senior Project Engineer, etc.," then follow with "You may be interested, etc.," listing accomplishments which pertain to the ad.

Here again, no personal characteristics or traits should be mentioned. The concluding sentence should be phrased as it was on your motivation letter. There should be no begging or pleas for replies.

In scanning for ads, the following sources are some of the best: The *Wall Street Journal* publishes four regional editions covering the U.S. The *New York Times*, especially the Sunday edition, also receives national exposure. The metropolitan papers offer mostly state coverage. Thus, if you desire, you have a geographic choice. Main public libraries usually have out-of-town major metropolitan newspapers.

Incidentally, newspapers can be checked several weeks after publication, since those ads are still live prospects. Trade publications in your field sometimes contain "Position Available" ads. These are the major sources for locating ads. You may know of others yourself.

As one of your "sales channels," ad responses are second only to the motivation letter. Therefore take advantage of this exposure to your marketplace by continuously searching for them.

CHAIN REFERRALS

Chain referral letters—such as the following examples—have proven successful in many instances. Some executives hesitate to use this approach because it involves friends, business associates or college classmates. However, chain referrals should be used since as complete an exposure as possible is necessary to locate the right position, and one never knows from which "sales channel" it will develop. *If you are unemployed, it definitely should be used.* Try to obtain 50 to 100 names for this purpose.

You may not have been in touch with some of these people for many years, during which time they are unaware of your background or accomplishments. You are not asking for a job in a chain referral letter. You are merely seeking advice and possible contacts for interviews.

The salutation should be the same as you would normally use in addressing the individual since this is a personal letter from you. For example: "Dear Robert" (or) "Dear Bob" (or) "Dear Mr. (Doctor, etc.) Jones." Following are two illustrations of the chain referral letter; the second one being the one you will send to people who have been referred to you. Note that resumes *are* enclosed with these letters.

Example I

REFERRAL LETTER

(To be typed on Personal Letterhead)

Name
Company
Address
City, State, Zip Code

Dear (first name - or as you would normally address him):

(If unemployed, state, "Due to conditions beyond my control, I am presently unemployed.")

(If employed, use this paragraph):
Very recently I decided to evaluate my business career. I have concluded that I can make better use of my qualifications elsewhere and therefore am seriously considering making a change.

Realizing the importance and influence of broad-scale contacts, I want to test the value of my background and experience as widely as possible in relation to the realities of the marketplace.

It occurred to me that within your circle of acquaintances, you might know of one or more persons who may be interested in receiving my resume. (Copy enclosed.) These contacts could be of inestimable value to me in developing a list of appropriate firms and executives to contact.

I would appreciate hearing from you, and will welcome any comments you may have about the resume. Naturally, I'd like you to keep this confidential. (Note: Omit last sentence, if unemployed).

                              Best personal wishes,

                                 (your name)

Example 2

REFERRAL LETTER

Referred By Friend

(To be typed on Personal Letterhead)

Name
Company
Address
City, State, Zip Code

Dear Mr. _____:

Mr. _____ of _____ has suggested that I contact you.

(If unemployed, state, "Due to conditions beyond my control, I am presently unemployed.")

(If employed, use this paragraph):
Very recently I decided to evaluate my business career. I have concluded that I can make better use of my qualifications elsewhere and therefore am seriously considering making a change.

Realizing the importance and influence of broad-scale contacts, I want to test the value of my background and experience as widely as possible, in relation to the realities of the marketplace.

Mr. _____ felt that within your circle of acquaintances, you might know one or more persons who may be interested in receiving my resume. (Copy enclosed.) These contacts could be of inestimable value to me in developing a list of appropriate firms and executives to contact.

I would appreciate hearing from you.

Sincerely,

(your name)

BUSINESS NEWS ITEMS

The *Wall Street Journal,* trade periodicals and the financial pages of newspapers are good sources for the "business news item" exposure in obtaining interviews. Although this approach may not be the most effective, it is another "sales channel" to be explored.

The following example of how a business news item letter might read will explain the purpose of this method for obtaining possible interviews.

BUSINESS NEWS ITEMS EXAMPLE

JOHN J. JONES
2345 Jarvis Boulevard
Port Smith, Ohio 22205
(123) 456 - 7890

January 2, 198__

Mr. R.L. Benson
Acme National Mfg. Co.
13422 Central Ave.
Cleveland, Ohio

Dear Mr. Benson:

The story in Monday's edition of the <u>Wall Street Journal</u> regarding your company's plans for expansion interests me greatly. I have been aware of Acme National progress for some time, and your plans for market expansion by building new plants to better service customers are another indication of your planning for the future.

It occurs to me that in your plans and expansion program you may have need for an executive with my background and abilities.

Young, age 41, I have a BS degree in Industrial Management and an MBA. Currently I am Chief Industrial Manager for a nationally-known consulting firm. (Note: If unemployed, state, "Due to conditions beyond my control, I am presently unemployed.")

In the course of my assignments, I have successfully interpreted and implemented programs towards developing volume and profit, while also serving to coordinate better long-range planning with scheduling of facilities, equipment and skills available or required.

I would be glad to meet with you to discuss how my experience and capabilities can make meaningful contributions in your company's continued growth.

Sincerely,

EXECUTIVE RECRUITERS

Some companies engage Executive Recruiters (Search Firms) to locate an executive in the middle or top management echelon. It behooves you, therefore, to contact the ones in your field as another "sales outlet." The chances are slight that they may be seeking an executive with your qualifications at that particular moment, but it is best not to pass up any potential.

The distance or time factor may prevent you from making a personal visit, but a letter contact is the next best step. However, as the third party intermediary, they must know all about you. In your letter state your present earnings and your salary range requirements since these are not included in your resume. *Enclose a "fact" sheet outlining every function you performed in each of your positions.* Send three resumes with accompanying fact sheets. Search firms need complete information for their corporate clients before any contacts are made with you.

There are many good executive recruiter firms, located primarily in the major cities. You can obtain their names from the out-of-town telephone directories available at your main telephone office.

EMPLOYMENT AGENCIES

Here, as with executive search firms, the possibilities are not too productive. However, some executives are placed through them and they should therefore be contacted.

Check those employment agencies which advertise for your type of career image. Visit them at their least busy time which is usually mid-afternoon and toward the end of the week. You may have to leave a few resumes, but include a fact sheet with each one.

Out-of-town employment agencies should be contacted by letter on the specific position advertised. Send a resume and fact sheet along.

ADVICE CALLS

It is relatively easy to obtain a meeting with a president or senior executive of a company, provided you seek advice and counsel only. They feel flattered that you selected them. Most people will offer advice so long as it does not cost them anything. No matter how busy a president may be, chances are good that he will make time for your visit.

The best approach is to phone the executive, introduce yourself, and say something to this effect: "I am considering making a career move and would appreciate it if you could spare ten to fifteen minutes to advise me whether or not I am heading in the right direction." Play it by ear from there. You will usually find that he will suggest the time for the meeting.

Do not ask him for a job. You did not meet him for this purpose. Explain what your plans are, and ask him for advice. He may offer you a position in his organization or suggest that you see certain individuals in other companies. He may be so impressed that he will personally arrange interviews for you, which has frequently occurred.

(*Note:* Bank presidents are also a good source for advice calls. They know what is going on in the business world of their community.)

In addition to being a potential sales outlet, "advice calls" answer another very important purpose of affording you opportunities for practice interviews. After several of these meetings, you become a more competent, assured and relaxed person, which will reflect itself into a positive attitude when you participate in actual interviews.

REFERENCES

You certainly would not submit a name as a reference unless you believed a good report would be forthcoming. However, many executives have lost potential positions because of adverse reference reports. You feel all references are your friends who will extol your capabilities and virtues. This is usually true, but every so often an uncomplimentary or lukewarm report is received by a prospective employer which prevents you from getting the job.

It is therefore best to know what your references will say about you before submitting their names. At least attempt to secure this information. However, very few companies will reveal the contents of the references to you.

There are several methods to obtain this information beforehand, but tact and diplomacy are required. One way is to contact your proposed references and request a "To Whom It May Concern" letter on their business stationery. This tends to obligate the reference to say the same things about you when contacted by a prospective employer. Also you can ask the reference to make some changes, should the reference be a negative one. (*Note:* Do not at any time use a "To Whom It May Concern" letter as a reference.)

Another method is the "third party" approach. This method may hurt your conscience somewhat, and although honesty is preferable in everything you do, this method can be condoned as a necessary "little white lie." In this instance, have an attorney friend send a letter requesting information about you. (See Example page 173.) Some career counseling firms use variations of this type of letter.

A third approach is to personally see each reference, if possible, advising that you are formulating a job campaign and would like to review details of your employment with which he may be unfamiliar. Then ask whether you may use his name as a reference. He may make suggestions which will give you an idea as to what he will say about you.

If practically possible, at least ten persons should be contacted in order to obtain the names of three or four which can be used at different times, depending on the particular applications. The same references should not be contacted so consistently that they become annoyed with you. *Do not offer or propose the names of references unless the company requests them.* References should not be contacted by companies unless there is an active interest expressed.

If it is necessary to furnish the name of a former employer with whom you are not on good terms, be honest with the prospective company and explain why an adverse type of reference may be sent. In any event, references often help you to attain or lose a desired position.

(*Note:* Once a reference is aware that you are seeking a position, it is possible that he may recommend you to his own company or other companies he knows. Thus, even "references" can become a sales outlet for your product.)

REFERENCE REQUEST EXAMPLE

Attorney's Letterhead

                                        Re: Mr. John J. Jones

Dear Mr.

We represent a company who is seeking an individual with the background and experience of the type possessed by the above-named gentleman in whom an interest has been expressed.

We would like to know more about him and would appreciate your comments concerning his character, over-all abilities and management qualifications.

                    Sincerely yours,

PERSONAL CONTACTS

Make as many personal contacts as possible. Although this may be a highly sensitive area for the sake of anonymity in some fields, if done cautiously it is a good sales outlet. People as a rule do not violate confidences, so do not hesitate to approach business associates, friends and even banks. Inquiries at trade association meetings or conventions will sometimes bring to light anticipated changes or present openings. Discreetly, you can make known that you are considering a change of position. *Of course, if you are unemployed, let the "whole world" know that you are seeking a position.*

ALUMNI PLACEMENT ORGANIZATIONS

Some colleges maintain excellent Alumni Placement departments, while others are relatively ineffective. This avenue should also be explored with an initial personal contact, if possible. After a conference leave a resume with the department, but ask that a position request be forwarded to you in order that you can make your own personal contact with the company. You, who are most concerned, can sell yourself better than the department can.

Write to the department if you are unable to make a visit. Enclose a resume, and here also, request the opportunity of making contact personally with any company inquiries. It is a good idea to keep in touch from time to time with the department to prevent your resume from getting lost in the shuffle.

PROFESSIONAL SOCIETIES

Professional societies in your field can also be of assistance. Many of them issue periodic "Situation Wanted" bulletins. Ask that you be listed in their bulletin, but try to write the copy yourself. In addition, register with those societies which have placement departments.

SITUATION WANTED ADS

A "Situation Wanted" ad in a major paper or trade publication may be run after all other methods have failed to produce the desired results. (Frankly, it is highly improbable that the need would arise for such an ad if all the other avenues have been fully explored.)

In running an ad, you have to be extremely fortunate to have all of the various timing elements in your favor. Even if a position is open, the company executive concerned may be away on a trip or vacation and will not get a chance to read your ad. Results are seldom productive, but you will receive a lot of junk mail.

Should you decide to run an ad, make it appealing. Read the display ads for "Position Available" and follow their pattern. (*Note:* Age, if mature, a salary figure, and any reference to a resume should be omitted. You are seeking interviews, and the mention of these particular items in the ad could be definite drawbacks.)

SUMMARY

We have covered the 12 following methods of exposure:

1. The Mailing
2. Answering Ads
3. Chain Referrals
4. Business News Items
5. Executive Recruiters
6. Employment Agencies
7. Advice Calls
8. References
9. Personal Contacts
10. Alumni Placement Organizations
11. Professional Societies
12. Situation Wanted Ads

As your own Marketing Manager, you should explore all these outlets to obtain the most complete coverage possible in the marketplace. Obviously, some avenues are more productive than others, but one never knows from which exposure will come the best offer to fit your individual need.

The motivation letter mailing to 100 or more companies is your best possibility to obtain the greatest number of interviews. Concentrate most effort on this approach; however, do not neglect the others at the expense of this one.

Your first and most important role is to obtain interviews, for without them no jobs can be gotten. You know the product and you have explored all the sales channels. Now at the interview you have to be a good enough salesman to "sell" the product. In other words, receive offers and line up those interviews. The greater the number of offers, the better your chances are to obtain a position.

Implementation of Marketing Campaign

INTERVIEW TECHNIQUES

The first obstacle has been overcome in the exposure of your product. You have an appointment with a potential buyer for your services. It's now up to you to sell him in order to obtain an offer. How well you do this selling at each interview will determine the number of offers received. Evaluations can then be made to select the company best suited for your career goal.

Thus far the interviewer knows very little about you. In fact, he may not even have your resume. Therefore, initial appearance impressions are important. Dress neatly in a business suit and not in casual clothes. (Career Women: see special chapter). Wear a regular tie, not a bow tie. (Some people associate bow ties with juveniles.) No fraternal society pins should be worn. Nothing flashy should appear. Let the people you meet remember you for your capabilities, and not as the "guy with the big diamond stickpin."

After the opening amenities have been covered and you are seated, do not slump in the chair, but sit naturally and comfortably. Look the interviewer straight in the eye *all the time,* for if you know your product, there will be no need to glance sideways, groping for an answer. Also, you will be in a position to watch his facial expressions for positive or negative reactions. Thus you can tell which way the interview is going and take remedial steps if necessary.

Don't fiddle around with anything in your hand. Act assured, not nervous. Even if ashtrays are present, always request permission to smoke.

Very few executives know how to interview prospective employees, for after all, this is not their profession. They may be just as apprehensive and nervous as you are. Whether they are or not, it is important that you take control of the interview. Information researched about the company in advance will give you knowledge in the type of questions to ask. (*Note:* Good sources for information about the company are stock brokerage firms, banks and business reference books such as *Dun & Bradstreet, Standard & Poor,* etc.)

Maintain a positive approach, but be careful that you do not become too aggressive or offensive. Act confidently in the knowledge of your product. The "advice calls" practice interviews will help to give you poise and confidence.

You are at the interview for two reasons only: you have a "problem," and the company has one too. The interviewer will try to find out all about your problem, and it is up to you to get to know his reasons for your being there. Sometimes you will be told without asking, and at other times, you will need to inquire subtly why the position is open.

A good point to remember: *You have lost nothing that you haven't had in the first place!* This attitude will give you greater confidence in yourself and cause less hesitancy or fear in asking questions. Any interviewer who resents your delving into the company's affairs represents a firm with which you should not be associated. Interviewers do not hesitate to dig in depth about you. Most executives appreciate your questioning and have greater respect for your ability to investigate situations or conditions in order to resolve a potential problem.

THE PORTFOLIO

The best interview aid or tool is a "portfolio" of yourself. A portfolio is a binder containing pertinent information about you, and serves a dual purpose. First, it acts as a reminder of your functions and accomplishments so that a glance at any page will immediately recall the subject matter to you. Thus you are on familiar home ground, and will feel more at ease during the interview.

Secondly, the portfolio becomes the physical product itself to the buyer. It is easier to sell a product if the buyer can examine it, rather than just hearing about it. The ashtray salesman referred to earlier will sell far more ashtrays by *showing* his product, rather than just describing it. Thus, when the interviewer asks what you have been doing, reply, "Let me show you what I've been doing," and bring out your portfolio from your briefcase. However, do not dwell on any one part at great length, unless questioned by the interviewer.

(*Note:* In the interview always carry just a small briefcase which contains your portfolio and some resumes. Do not scare the interviewer by bringing in large cases full of voluminous material.)

The portfolio is simple to prepare. However, since it is your sample case, it should be neatly arranged. Purchase a good binder which can hold a number of oversize 9" x 11" acetate pockets. Standard letter size pages are 8 1/2" x 11", therefore your material can be inserted into these pockets, making an attractive appearance. It is easier, too, for instant removal of individual pieces when necessary.

Nothing of a highly confidential or classified nature should ever be part of your portfolio. You can assemble letters addressed to you or from you, showing your titles and functions; an organizational chart listing your position (create one, if none is available); pictures of products or projects in which you were involved, especially if you are in a technical field (some companies produce brochures of their products from which you can extract parts associated with you); financial reports or statements if pertinent; newspaper or company publication items about you connected with company affairs; merit awards; and any other job-associated information which can be included.

(*Note:* Only photocopies of valuable personal papers, not the originals, should be inserted as a protection in case the portfolio is lost.)

You may not be a scrapbook type saver, but most people keep some papers. Your spouse may have put these things away, so ask for assistance in the search. If you are presently employed, it is easier to obtain most material. Previous employment material may be more difficult, but there too, brochures, statements, etc., are usually available.

Wherever possible, organize the portfolio by companies with whom you were associated, showing your present or latest company first. You may include a small section in the back of the portfolio of civic activities. Some companies, especially in smaller communities, appreciate the goodwill created for them by executives who are civic-minded.

Turn the portfolio away from you and have it face the interviewer when you lay it on the desk, turning the pages while reading upside down. In order to do this, you must know what is in the portfolio and where to locate a specific item without any fumbling. The portfolio is your physical product and a good salesman *knows* his product.

The portfolio should contain no more than ten double-sided pages, for it need not be bulky to be effective.

TIPS AND PITFALLS

Most of the time you have to play the interview by ear. However, you should expect the usual standard questions:

"What have you been doing?" or "Tell me about yourself." If possible, start with the portfolio and say, "Let me show you what I've been doing." You must ask questions as you go along, as for example, "How does this activity fit in with your needs?" This will get the interviewer to talk, which is what you want most. The more he speaks due to your direction, the more knowledgeable you will become as to why you are there. Then you will know how to respond to his needs where you are best qualified, and inject your strength at his weakest points. The interviewer will hopefully decide that you are the man who can resolve his problems.

"Why do you want to leave your company?" or "Why do you want to change your position?" *Don't ever belittle your present or previous employers, regardless of the situation or circumstances involved;* no one likes to have a disgruntled person around. Start off by praising the company and its personnel: "I like my company and the people with whom I am associated, and have given considerable thought to leaving. However, because of the conservative nature of the company, I feel that all of my capabilities and potential are not being fully utilized." Or, "because it is family-owned there is little opportunity for advancement." Or, "because of a merger some of my functions were delegated to others, thereby reducing my policy-making activities," etc.

"What are your salary requirements?" or "What would you be willing to start at?" or some other form of question on this subject. Your best answer involves *no commitment* by you. Once you mention an amount, you have eliminated all chances for negotiating salary. If you state a figure, it may be too low and the interviewer may feel you are too "light" for the job; or the company could be getting a bargain since they expected to pay more. If the figure is too high, you may be too "heavy" for the company. Once you start at a low figure, you cannot go back later and claim that the salary is too low for the responsibilities involved. You can be told that the amount decided on was the one you wanted.

Therefore, the best time to negotiate is at the time the question is raised. (*Note:* Some firms have established policies on starting salaries and will tell you so. In this event there is little you can do.)

The correct answer to the question is to throw it back into the interviewer's lap. *"Mr. Jones, salary is negotiable. I'm primarily interested in a career opportunity by proving what I can do for the company. By the way, what is the salary range for the position we're discussing?"* Now it's his turn. He may ask you how much you are earning, and your answer has to be truthful, but always add a "plus" after the figure, such as $25,000 plus. There's always a plus, even if it is a gift at Christmas time.

Note the word "range" in your answer. It is a very important word. If you asked what the position "pays," he could answer a specific amount, say $20,000. By using the word "range" you are asking him to give his low and high figure. He could say $20,000 to $30,000, which would give a bargaining figure.

At this point do not raise the subject of fringe benefits. When the company feels that they want you and make a firm offer, then discuss fringe benefits. (*Note:* Sometimes fringe benefits are disclosed to you at the time of the offer.) Individual fringe benefits, besides the regular company policy plans, include such items as relocation expense, living allowance for you while looking for a place to live before the family moves, stock options, salary increases, deferred salaries, contracts, etc.

You may be taken to lunch outside the company plant. It is best to refuse a cocktail at lunch time. Give some excuse for not accepting, such as not making it a habit to drink during the day. If invited to dinner, then *one and only one* cocktail should be ordered. Most people are only social drinkers. After a full day's tension at an interview, more than one drink could very well cause you to become a blabbermouth, which is the last thing you want to be. Also, companies sometimes try to get you to take a few drinks as a test of how well you conduct yourself. You may represent the company image in a community and they want to be certain that you will not tarnish it.

Make it a "must" to visit the plant or operation. See for yourself whether modern equipment is used and what the working conditions are. You want to meet the individual to whom you will report. Is he your type of person? Does he give any indication that his job is in jeopardy because of you? You certainly don't want any strikes against you once you accept the position.

Be sure to inquire if the position is open due to an advancement or resignation, unless the position is newly created. If it is open because of a release or resignation, find out how long the man was in this position. If just a short time, ask how long the previous incumbent had the position. You may discover that several persons held this job during a few short years. A large turnover could mean that the company is a difficult one to get along with, and therefore you want no part of it.

Advancement causing the opening is a healthy sign. However, find out why there was no one within the organization to fill the opening. You may run into some back-stabbing by a disgruntled individual who felt that the position should have been offered to him.

Do not raise the subject of expenses for your trip during the interview. However at the end of the interview, if the interviewer has made no mention of it, say "Oh, by the way, to whom should I submit my expense statement?"

If the interview was arranged by phone, state at the end of the call to the caller, "Of course the company will pay expenses." Make it a positive statement and you will receive a positive reply. However, if the trip is a short one, forget about the small expense involved.

If the interview entails an overnight trip, ask the caller to make hotel accommodations for you at the place where they usually put up guests. The hotel normally bills the company and your expense statement will be less. Usually, the company will arrange to pick you up at the hotel and take you to their offices.

Before you accept a position, especially in a small town, have your family visit the area to determine if they will be happy in the community. Homes, schools, stores, etc. are important factors in your appraisal of the position. Many companies will pay for your and your spouse's expenses—if you ask. These trips should be arranged for weekends if possible.

At the end of the interview try to obtain a definite return date, if no offer has been made. If the interviewers say, "We will let you know," it's up to you to ask "By what date?" They are apparently stalling for time because they have other candidates in mind or want further time to discuss you among themselves. By obtaining a definite return date you are saying in effect that you don't want to be stalled too long. Don't be afraid to be positive about asking for a prompt decision, for you then appear to be a decision maker yourself. You can always afford to be positive in your attitude. You have everything to gain and nothing to lose.

A resume should be left with the company after the interview is ended. After meeting with you, a resume will help recall pertinent facts about you.

INTERVIEW FOLLOW-UP LETTER

A follow-up letter should be sent after each interview which thanks the interviewer for the courtesies extended and acknowledges by name the people you have met. Briefly recap the discussions in terms of particulars concerning the position and how you would fit into the organization. Don't write anything mushy, but rather stick to facts. Another reason is furnished for writing if the company asked you to submit your expense statement.

Regular Follow-Ups

If you don't hear from the company as arranged, call to find out whether or not a decision has been reached. Usually it is better to use the phone whenever you can, rather than to write. Frankly, if you are stalled too often indicating that a decision has not been made, forget that company. A company that takes a long time in making a decision is not the right one for you.

PRACTICE INTERVIEWS

In addition to obtaining leads for exposure, "advice calls" were also covered for the sake of making practice interviews, which give you poise and confidence when participating in actual ones.

Another good practice interview method is to have your spouse or a friend read the "Interview" section of this book. Then let her or him become the "interviewer" from the opening of the interview until the close. These role-playing sessions will teach you the right answers and the significant questions to ask. Your spouse or friend can help to make you a "pro" not only in interview techniques, but in the entire field of seeking a job, or career advancement, by acting as a sounding board.

STALLING AN OFFER

On the assumption that an offer was made, it is essential that you stall acceptance until you have had an opportunity to evaluate other offers. Acknowledge every offer at the time you receive it by saying something to this effect, "Thank you, Mr. Jones, for feeling that I can contribute to your management team. I would certainly appreciate the privilege of becoming associated with your company. However, I do wish to think it over;" or "discuss it with my family;" or "I have two more interviews arranged and I'd like to talk with them before I make a final decision, although at this point I feel that your company offers the greatest opportunities."

INTERVIEW REPORT FORM

No matter how well the interview progressed, fill out an "Interview Report Form" (see example) immediately after leaving the premises. If the interview was of short duration—an hour or so—it went badly and you may as well forget about an offer. However, by filling out the "interview report form" you can avoid making the same mistakes in future interviews. Even if the interview was a good one, the form will indicate how you can improve or perhaps point out your stronger assets.

Pretend you are a salesman working for a company that requires reports of your activities. The "interview report form" actually serves three purposes: First, it acts as a guide in the type of questions to ask. Second, it is a self-improvement form in interview technique. Third, it will make it easier to recall your visits in the evaluation of offers for a final choice.

Interview Report

Company . . . . Date. . . . .

Address & phone. . . . .

Interviewed by . . . .

Other individuals seen . . . .

. . . .

Type of person (Immediate superior). . . . .

Products produced . . . .

Sales volume . . . .

Methods of distribution . . . .

Position discussed . . . .

Responsibilities and requirements . . . .

. . . .

Other openings . . . .

Company problems . . . .

. . . .

Comments on interview . . . .

. . . .

. . . .

Results of interview . . . .

. . . .

Follow-up action planned . . . .

. . . .

SUMMARY

To paraphrase President Kennedy, "It is not what the company can do for you, but what you can do for the company" which the interviewer is most concerned about. The more you can prove your worth, the better are your chances for receiving an offer. You have made a "sale" if an offer has been tendered.

Evaluation of Final Offers

Throw all the offers, including your present company and position, into an imaginary hopper. Compare each one against the personal assessment which you made earlier. Relate the offers to your personality and career needs, growth potential and geographic location for fulfillment of goals. *Although immediate income is an important economic factor, make it a secondary consideration in your decision,* provided you are assured that if you produce, the opportunities exist for higher positions with increased income.

Occasionally, it is possible that after a complete search has been made, you will decide that the outside world has less to offer than your own company. You couldn't have known this before, and your mind would not have been at ease had you not tried. If this is the case and you decide to remain in your present job, then change your attitude toward your company, your superiors and your associates. You may discover that you, not they, were most at fault. Suddenly you may realize that their attitude toward you has changed as well, and you will be working happily in a harmonious atmosphere.

When you have evaluated all the offers including the alternative of remaining with your own company, the one that comes out from the tip of the hopper is the one best suited for you. Accept it!

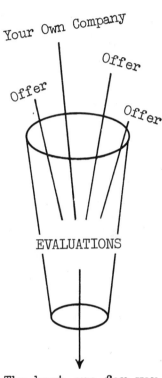

The best one for you.

ADDITIONAL THOUGHTS

Hopefully you may find, as many others have, that you will be offered a better position than the one for which you have been interviewed. The manner in which you have presented yourself and your capabilities open up new areas in the minds of the president or senior executive whereby you could take over some of their burdens and responsibilities in a different and higher position.

Obtaining time off for interviews may be somewhat difficult for employed people. It is best, therefore, to arrange or postpone your vacation to tie in with your marketing schedule for interviews. As an executive you should be able to take a day off occasionally with or without a reason. However, vacation time should be utilized when several days are required for interviews.

Should you be unemployed during the campaign, try to obtain any sort of interim or temporary job, even as a clerk in a store. The job doesn't matter as long as you don't just hang around the house. Don't let your pride stand in the way. Any defeatist attitude will reflect itself in your demeanor and appearance and in your interviews when you most need a positive approach.

Set aside a certain percentage of your salary, as little as 1%, as a job contingency fund. As with a Christmas Savings Club account, cash will be available when most needed. It will help to tide you over and afford you the courage to wait until the "right" job is offered.

POSITION RE-EVALUATION

No matter what echelon position you obtain, the company is taking a gamble on your services and your performance will be gauged or measured during the first three months' probation period.

Similarly, during the first three months on the job, re-evaluate the company to determine if promises are kept and working conditions as you expected. Is it the right company for you?

Despite the fact that you have probed, screened and assessed the company in advance, there still is the human element error factor involved. If it is not the right company, you certainly do not want to continue an unhappy business marriage, so revive and resurrect the other offers while still on the job, and while the other offers are possibly fresh. (*Note:* This is one reason why you should not accept the first offer of a job. Stall until you obtain several offers.)

It is a rare case when the company proves to be the wrong one. What this re-evaluation will really do is to set you thinking what you can and should do for the company and yourself to better your efforts for greater future success.

For the Career Woman

There have been recent positive changes in employers' attitudes toward women executives. The job market for career women has therefore greatly expanded—which is certainly a welcome improvement over previous discriminatory practices. More openings exist now than ever before.

However, there are still a lot of die-hard employers who feel that a highly responsible position should be a male exclusive. The age-old obstacles of marriage, childbirth, wishes of a husband, etc. are the usual reasons for their selection of a male applicant over a potentially more capable female. Hiring and training are costly expenses when turnover versus longevity is considered by employers.

Apparently, some women have considerable trouble in convincing a prospective employer to grant an interview and, if one is received, they fail to obtain the position open. The first requirement or immediate goal is, of course, to get the interview, and this is strongly stressed throughout the book. It is then necessary to do a selling job (of yourself) at the interview.

The usual arguments or approaches to overcome the objections are often inadequate or insufficient. Following, therefore, are some additional guidelines and suggestions which have proven successful in a great number of instances:

Stress in both your Motivation letters and at your interviews that you are a *career person*. Your letters should start with, "I am a career woman in the field of Marketing" (or whatever your field may be). Then go on from there with the regular form of Motivation letter you are using. This initial statement immediately tends to remove the unfair stigma attached to women executives concerning longevity of employment.

At the interviews it is best to remark right at the start something to this effect: "Mr. Jones, I would like you to know that I am primarily interested in a career opportunity with your organization. I want to grow with the company." This statement, too, implies longevity of service.

Let the interviewer see you as the most capable person to fill the opening, rather than as a female applicant. In other words, play down your gender and stress the position qualifications you possess.

Forget or disregard the problematic female drawbacks or handicaps in your approach to a prospective employer. This mental sensitivity could reflect itself in a negative attitude which is easily transmitted to the interviewer. Anticipate and expect them to hire you for your ability to make a profit for the company.

Personal circumstances may sometimes necessitate a local geographic area limitation which makes it difficult to find and obtain the best position for you. If possible, enlarge your area when making your search. Then you can state in your resume that you are willing to relocate and (some) travel if you are so inclined.

(Note that the resumes for men in this book can be converted to your fields, since the principles and resume styles are identical.)

Dress conservatively, in good taste, at interviews. After employment one can dress as befits the custom of the organization.

In summary, women are now in a more favorable position for executive employment than ever before. More and more women are listed as members on the Boards of Directors of some of the largest companies in this country. Your opportunities are limitless; take advantage of them as the percentage of women executives rises sharply in the world of business and industry.

Longevity and Advancement

You have successfully applied the methods described in this book and have obtained a position. Good! The next objective is to retain the position for the sake of longevity and to progress or advance within the structure of the company.

Several basic principles are involved to attain these goals. In order to remain with your company, your *performance* is a major factor for recognition. This is a definite consideration at each job-evaluation time, for obtaining pay increases as well as for indicating one's progress.

There is a proven formula which spells success in "performance." Its symbol is "AMP", which represents:

$$\underline{ABILITY} + \underline{MOTIVATION} = \underline{PERFORMANCE}$$

ABILITY is *Know-how*. If you know, understand and are capable of doing your job, you have the Ability. (If not, then take advantage of additional schooling, trade journals, seminars, etc. to increase your knowledge.) You must show that you possess Ability in the position for which you were hired.

MOTIVATION is the *Willingness*, the *Desire* to apply this Ability to the fullest extent. The old cliché that "The road to hell is paved with good intentions" aptly reflects itself here. What good is it to know *how* if you don't follow through? You may plan on getting a job done on time, but you procrastinate. Then the job is either late in accomplishment or never fully completed.

PERFORMANCE becomes the *Result* of utilizing knowledgeable Ability with ambitious Motivation. Follow the "AMP" formula and your tenure will be secure. In other words, justify your job. In the Preface, we state that an employer must realize a profit from your services, otherwise he doesn't need or can't afford you. This applies to any function within an organization, whether it is a "staff" (office) of a "line" (operation) position.

"APEN"

There is also a wordplay called "APEN" which will aid you in maintaining longevity. It stands for: *A*ccentuate the *P*ositive, *E*liminate the *N*egative. This doesn't mean that you should be too aggressive, argumentative, dogmatic, opinionated, etc., but rather that you should learn to speak and act *positively* in your presentations and demeanor. Your performance, ideas and suggestions will be accepted in a positive manner.

For example, you can ask the *same* question in two different ways. One will get you a positive "yes" response; the other will return a negative "no" reply.

"This pencil writes very easily, doesn't it?" (A "yes" reply)
"This pencil doesn't write very easily, does it?" (A "no" reply)

—therefore—

"Always phrase a question to obtain a positive answer!"
"Never phrase a question to get a negative answer!"

Note that the above two sentences are identical in meaning. Which one is preferable? If you are positive, you eliminate self-defeatism in your thinking and actions.

Another good principle: *"BE A STEMWINDER!"* A watch that doesn't run is of no value for its purpose to tell time. A dollar watch that is wound to keep time is better than an unwound thousand dollar watch, insofar as utility is concerned. In order to keep things going, a person should, therefore, be a "Stemwinder." Be active, alert and make things happen. You will be recognized and rewarded for your efforts.

There is an old saying that there are three types of workers:

One who makes things happen (A Stemwinder)
One who watches things happen (and)
One who doesn't know what happened

The #1 type will not only build longevity with the company but will advance to a higher position as openings occur or are created. The #2 type will usually hide himself in a corner somewhere and possibly have some length of service, but he stands little chance for advancement. The #3 type will be what the job market considers a person who is first in line to be dismissed when the occasion arrises. Eventually, he has to seek many, and sometimes lesser, jobs during his working years.

WHAT IS AN EMPLOYEE WORTH?

What do you do when not busy on the job? Is there something useful which you can do? Make yourself as indispensable as possible. Learn new skills pertaining to the company's needs. Make suggestions; offer ideas; be an achiever; a problem solver. When a higher opening occurs, you should be the #1 choice to fill the vacancy.

Everything is easy if you know how. A baffling illusion to an audience is a simple deceptive trick for the magician, only because he has the know-how to perform it. One of the questions in the Self-Analysis section of this book is relevant here: "Knowing what the job requirements are, would you hire yourself if you were the employer?"

An employer expects you to improve yourself so that you will be of more value to the firm. Some companies even pay for total schooling or subsidize the tuition in order for the employee to become more proficient. Obviously, this added knowledge increases the potential for advancement and greater earning power.

Make it the kind of job where you look forward to going to work in the morning and hate to leave it at closing time! Your longevity will be secure with excellent opportunities for advancement.

The author started merely as a retail store vacuum cleaner salesman on a commission basis with Sears Roebuck & Co. Ultimately, he rose to the position of National Mail-Order Sales Manager of most major appliance divisions, by applying the principles outlined in this chapter.

Job Related Stress

There are numerous books published on psychological and physiological areas of stress authored by eminent professors and doctors. However, they mostly delve into the deeper recesses of human behavior.

As a layperson, it is sometimes difficult to comprehend the terminology and technical aspects of these treatises on the subject of stress and how they directly relate to an individual in a work situation.

The simplest definition of job stress is the mental, physical and emotional strain, tension, pressure, worry, apprehension and aggravation which a person encounters at work.

Conditions causing stress are too numerous to be listed in this chapter. However, the following is a brief summary of a few major situations in which stress occurs. Understanding and overcoming these pitfalls will assist in reducing and eliminating some of the stress which a job-holder experiences. Regardless of the type of work one does, whether it is a management position or not, stress is often the cause of many ailments, both physical and emotional, which affect job performance.

Have your children ever complained that they were too sick to go to school in the morning? Actually, they most likely faked the illness because they had to take a test that day and were afraid of it; or they had a bad experience the day before which preyed on their mind and they didn't wish to brave it again.

Just as children feign illness to avoid facing a reality, so have each one of us, at one time or another, decided to remain home rather than going to work that day. We, too, pretended we were "sick", supposedly, in order to escape temporarily from whatever job-related perplexities that were bothering us.

When stress rises to the point where it becomes unbearable, it is often a good idea, if possible, to take a one-day vacation from it. It may be helpful therapy to clear your mind of business problems for the day. You will return to your job the following morning in a fresh mood, ready to approach and tackle them.

Engaging in a hobby is also advisable therapy to reduce stress, since this activity causes you to completely forget, for the time being, whatever problems were disturbing you.

One area where stress is prevalent appears when subordinates or co-workers are advanced to better positions, while the individual remains "plateaued" in the same job. Frustration occurs, which becomes stress in this situation. In the section on "Long-Range Objectives" on page 22, the last sentence states emphatically that *"Job satisfaction is greatly dependent on your long-range goals, but must be assessed in self-acknowledged realistic terms."* Don't seek a goal higher than you can attain.

In other words, we sometimes overestimate our abilities and unrealistically believe we are qualified for a better position. This does not necessarily mean that the bypassed individual is not qualified or deserving of the promotion. However, in a large organization, one may be well-qualified, but not "politically oriented" and, therefore, overlooked for advancement. If this is the nature or character of the person (and incidentally, it is not wrong to be this way), then that person belongs in a smaller-sized company where top management is in closer contact with employees. Everyone there relates on a more personal basis and being a "politician" is less of a factor in obtaining rewards.

Stress also exists in large part when employees fail to understand the reasons for the behavior of superiors and/or co-workers. One doesn't need to be a psychologist to realize why they act as they do. Simple reasoning will tell you why. We sometimes overreact to incidents of little significance and magnify them out of proportion to the occurrence. They, like you, may have personal or, unknown to you, business pressure problems which bring to bear on their attitudes and actions.

A good policy is to leave your personal problems on the doorstep of your company when you arrive for work in the morning. Do not bring them inside with you. Keeping your mind on them will cause your performance to suffer. By the same token, leave your business problems inside the company on your way home at closing time. Don't bring them home with you. You will appreciate a relaxing evening at home, thus enjoying your family while experiencing a relief and a release from business cares and stress.

Learn to control the emotions which tend to sap your vitality at work. For example, you are not about to change policies of the company which you find are objectionable. Once you have tried and haven't succeeded, don't knock your head against a brick wall, so to speak. Try to understand why they exist, accept them, live with them, or else seek other employment. This will help to overcome the stress under which you may be laboring.

We hear rumors and give credence to them. We frequently jump to conclusions which we later find are erroneous. It is best to examine all the facts first. Unnecessary, worrisome stress results from wrong interpretations of idle gossip and unsubstantiated rumors.

Be a team player! Sometimes a suggestion you have made or an idea you presented was not accepted at the time. Later, the same idea or suggestion was proposed by the superior, to whom you originally gave it, and offered to the company as his own. This often occurs in large companies. Obviously, it is for the benefit of the company and, if accepted, all gain by it. In the future, however, make sure that your proposal is in written form so that a dated record of it is maintained. Meanwhile, try to release from you mind the injustice of the incident. There's no sense in continuously thinking and fretting over it. The aggravation could make you ill.

Then there is the egotistical superior. He usually has an inferiority complex and must assert or demonstrate his authority by behaving in a demeaning manner towards an employee, often in front of other people. This is degrading to the employee and is a definite cause for depression/stress. Sometimes an order is given, advice offered or a reprimand made in an arbitrary loud tone of voice which is offensive to the employee.

The best method to overcome these and similar types of stress, is to leave the room afterwards and *"blow your stack"*. Release all the animosity from your system without anyone around. Call this individual every name you can think of. Get the incident off your chest. You will feel better when you return to work. Your "cool" will be back too. Don't let it get to you. Realize the source of the aggravation. Forget the episode as though it never occurred.

You and others who may have been there at the time understand this type of individual and agree that the unfairness of the method used was embarrassing to them as well. Similarly, some people will go to the piano and bang away on it for several minutes to rid themselves of their frustrations. They then return to a normal composure, thereby reducing the annoying stress they were suffering from.

None of us is perfect. We often unwittingly invite or encourage stress because we fail to relate to others or interact with them. This is especially true for the person who is a superior with jurisdiction over other employees. Knowing and understanding oneself will help to eliminate stress. This will result in better performance on the job.

Refer to page 18 in the "Self-Assessment" section under the heading, "Your Personality Traits and Characteristics". A reappraisal at this time would be very beneficial in determining who you really are and what you should do to improve your personality strengths and correct your weaknesses.

Of course, no job is worth becoming demoralized or getting sick over. However, if the job is desirable, then by understanding the reasons which are causing the stress, it is possible to reduce and/or overcome them.

The illustrations listed above are but a few of the many stress-causing situations. We feel, however, that they are the major job-related ones. We hope that the guidelines mentioned will help you to correct them. You then will be happier and more productive in your association with the company.

Conclusion

All successful marketing plans require a lot of intelligent thought and sincere effort. Your job search or career advancement campaign is no different. It will result in a most meaningful, satisfying and rewarding position with growth potential, provided you have followed the instructions in this Self-Marketing Guide.

Every known avenue has been explored. Proven methods of exposure, presentation and techniques have been explained as simply as possible for better comprehension, absorption and implementation. You now have the know-how, but you must apply it to attain the desired results. The chapters on Longevity and Advancement and Job-Related Stress should assist you in realizing complete job satisfaction, once you have obtained a position.

We sincerely hope the advice and counsel presented in this book will prove highly productive for you.

ABOUT THE AUTHOR

The author was involved for many years in career consulting, both as senior vice-president of a national executive consulting firm and later as the head of his own consulting company. Mr. Shykind was also National Mail Order Sales Manager of the appliance division of Sears, Roebuck and Company and Sales Promotion Manager of Spiegel, Inc., where he played a key role in the growth of its catalog order stores from 20 to 250. He has lectured and taught adult classes at Pima College and lectured at the University of Arizona to graduate and adult students on jobs and careers. He served as vice-president of the board of the Chicago School for Retarded Children. Mr. Shykind received his education at Western Reserve University.

ARCO Job-Finding Guides

YOUR JOB—WHERE TO FIND IT, HOW TO GET IT

Leonard Corwen. The complete guide to finding where the jobs are, using classified advertising, discovering and tapping the hidden job market, choosing personnel agencies and executive search firms, preparing resumes, and taking interviews.
ISBN 0-668-05131-0 Paper $6.95

HOW TO FIND AND LAND YOUR FIRST FULL-TIME JOB

Leonard Corwen. Expert advice for the first-time job-seeker from application to the first days on the job. Includes descriptions of over 300 occupations, list of helpful guides and directories, and salary charts.
ISBN 0-668-05463-8 Paper $4.95

RESUMES THAT GET JOBS

Resume Service. Over 70 model resumes for the jobs of the 80's. Job-seeking strategies, resume-writing hints, and interview techniques.
ISBN 0-668-05210-4 Paper $3.95

YOUR RESUME—KEY TO A BETTER JOB

Leonard Corwen. Everything you need to know to decide what kind of job you want, prepare a resume that will sell your special capabilities, and plan your job-hunting campaign.
ISBN 0-668-03733-4 Paper $4.00

HOW TO PASS EMPLOYMENT TESTS

Arco Editorial Board. An inside view of the employment tests used to screen applicants for a wide variety of jobs in private industry. Extensive practice with the kinds of questions used to determine clerical, stenographic, verbal, mechanical, or reasoning ability as well as those designed to measure supervisory or professional knowledge.
ISBN 0-668-05537-5 Paper $6.95

JOB HUNTER'S HANDBOOK: How to Sell Yourself and Get the Job You Really Want

Leonard Corwen. Expert and enlightening guide to doing the right thing at the right time to get you that perfect job!
ISBN 0-668-03877-2 Paper $1.75

For book ordering information refer to the last page of this book.

ORDER THE BOOKS DESCRIBED ON THE PREVIOUS PAGE FROM YOUR BOOKSELLER OR DIRECTLY FROM:

ARCO PUBLISHING, INC.
215 Park Avenue South
New York, N.Y. 10003

To order directly from Arco, please add $1.00 for first book and 35¢ for each additional book for packing and mailing cost. No C.O.D.'s accepted.

Residents of New York, New Jersey and California must add appropriate sales tax.

MAIL THIS COUPON TODAY!

ARCO PUBLISHING, INC., 215 Park Avenue South, New York, N.Y. 10003
Please rush the following Arco books:

NO. OF COPIES	TITLE #	TITLE	PRICE	EXTENSION
			SUB-TOTAL	
			LOCAL TAX	
			PACKING & MAILING	
			TOTAL	

I enclose check ☐, M.O. ☐ for $ _____
☐ Is there an Arco Book on any of the following subjects: _____
☐ Please send me your free Complete Catalog.

NAME _____

ADDRESS _____

CITY _____ STATE _____ ZIP _____

Every Arco book is guaranteed. Return for full refund within ten days if not completely satisfied.

NOT RESPONSIBLE FOR CASH SENT THROUGH THE MAILS

EP105

JAMES B. DUKE MEMORIAL LIBRARY
JOHNSON C. SMITH UNIVERSITY
CHARLOTTE, N. C. 26216